The Monty Hall Dilemma

Additional books

A Most Human Enterprise
by Donald Granberg and John F. Galliher

Social Judgment and Intergroup Relations:
Essays in Honor of Muzafer Sherif
Donald Granberg and Gian Sarup, Editors

The Political System Matters: Social Psychology and Voting Behavior
in Sweden and the United States
by Donald Granberg and Sören Holmberg

THE MONTY HALL DILEMMA:

A Cognitive Illusion *Par Excellence*

Donald Granberg

Lumad Publishing
Salt Lake City

Donald Granberg is professor emeritus of sociology at the University of Missouri Columbia. He is co-author with John F. Galliher of *A Most Human Enterprise: Controversies in the Social Sciences* published by Rowman and Littlefield, co-author with Sören Holmberg of *The Political System Matters: Social Psychology and Voting Behavior in Sweden and the United States* published by Cambridge University Press, and co-editor with Gian Sarup of *Social Judgment and Intergroup Relations: Essays in Honor of Muzafer Sherif* published by Springer-Verlag.

Professor Granberg has published articles in numerous sociology, psychology and political science journals.

Lumad Press 84108
Lumad Press, Salt Lake City
© 2014 by Lumad Publishing
All rights reserved. Published 2014
Printed in the United States of America

ISBN-13: 9780996100809
ISBN-10: 0996100806
Library of Congress Control Number: 2014906811
Lumad Publishing, Salt Lake City, UT
Ask Marilyn columns are reprinted with permission from PARADE Publications.
Excerpts from B. Schechter, *My Brain is Open: The Mathematical Journeys of Paul Erdös*, (New York: Simon and Schuster, 1998), 107-109, are reprinted with permission.
Letters to the Editor, "A Problem in Probability" and "On the Monty Hall Problem" printed in *The American Statistician*, 29, No. 1 (1975): 67 and 29, No. 3 (1975): 134 respectively are reprinted with permission from Taylor & Frances and Steve Selvin.

Dedicated to the Memory of Edith Emery

Mathematics Teacher
Willmar High School, Willmar, Minnesota

Acknowledgements

Thad Brown first introduced me to the Monty Hall Dilemma, together with his full measure of enthusiasm. In the words of Gardner Murphy, Thad was the hop toad, and I was the inch worm.

Upon my request, Marilyn vos Savant arranged for ten boxes of letters pertaining to the Monty Hall illusion, to be delivered to my office at the Center for Research in Social Behavior. I hope it is apparent that my level of understanding increased because of my having access to those letters.

A debt of thanks is owed for crucial insights provided by valued colleagues including Craig Anderson, Peter Mueser, and Jonah Schupbach.

It was Bertrand Granberg who persuaded us to consider self-publication and have the manuscript printed by CreateSpace, An Amazon.com Company. Bertrand Granberg, Douglas Wellman and John P. Wellman provided careful reading and amendment of *The Monty Hall Dilemma*.

Last but by no means least, many was the time when I exclaimed, "Beth, I need your help." She actually took charge of preparing this manuscript for publication. So to her, I offer my sincere and heartfelt thanks.

Table of Contents

PART THREE:
Odds and Ends

The Monty Hall Dilemma: A Cognitive Illusion *Par Excellence*.

INTRODUCTION

- A baseball manager tentatively decides to change pitchers. He saunters out to the mound, but before he signals a final decision he solicits advice from the pitcher and the catcher.

- An undergraduate student is taking a multiple choice exam, and gets stuck on number 37. She complains to the proctor that the item seems ambiguous. The proctor replies, "I see your point. I can rectify the situation by telling you that the correct answer to item 37 is **not** distracter B." In light of this new information, the student then proceeds to answer item 37.

- A man intends to propose marriage to a woman, and secretly buys an engagement ring. On their next date the couple falls into a pattern of seriously arguing over trivial matters. The man decides the mood is not right.

- The Commander of Allied Forces has to set a date and time for the Allied Forces to attack German forces on the mainland of France. He makes a decision to launch the attack based on the best information that he has at the time. He continues to monitor information regarding the weather and the tides, until at some point his decision becomes final and irrevocable.

These scenarios, though differing greatly in consequentiality, share in common the fact that they deal with decision making in stages. The category of **two stage decisions** is very large indeed, but the above examples should not be confused with our focal category of **Monty Hall Dilemmas**. For the latter to be appropriately labeled, it must meet the assumptions stated in Chapter 1.

Without passing judgment, there may be a continuum on which people fall, depending upon their proclivity to stick with a tentative decision, regardless of new evidence. At the opposite pole is *homo protean* who readily assumes various forms, depending on which way the wind blows.

Perhaps virtue falls somewhere in between. But consider this description of the persona many scholars think is our greatest president:

> Lincoln became known for his resolution. Once he made a decision, he stuck with it—a matter of no small importance when the issues became Union or Disunion, Victory or Defeat, Slavery or Freedom. As Lincoln once said to prominent political leaders who urged him to back away from the Emancipation Proclamation or face possible defeat for reelection in 1864: "The promise, once made, must be kept."[1]

Perhaps it is not so simple to see if the foregoing principle applies. **A cognitive illusion** occurs when the obvious answer to a thought question

---

1 J. McPherson, "Lincoln's Herndon." **The New York Review of Books**, March 26, 1998, **45**, No. 5, p.8.

turns out to be incorrect. Psychological reality conflicts with objective reality.

Knowing about cognitive illusions in general and the Monty Hall Dilemma in particular may foster an understanding of how cognitive illusions work. This should lead people to be alert to the possibility that ordinary reasoning and common sense don't always apply. As a consequence, they may become less dogmatic in their approach to everyday problems.

Chapter 2 contains several examples of cognitive illusions, "cousins" of the Monty Hall Dilemma. This chapter serves as stimulus to encourage the reader to start thinking in terms of the possibility that there may be something to this concept of cognitive illusion. By the criterion of parsimony, the Monty Hall Dilemma may be regarded as the cognitive illusion *par excellence*.

Chapter 3 presents letters written by people who became sufficiently motivated and, in many cases, upset about a popular columnist's analysis of the Monty Hall Dilemma. Succeeding chapters consist of surveys and experiments in which people are confronted with a Monty Hall Dilemma to see how they would actually choose. The working hypothesis was that people would show a strong tendency to stick with a tentative answer when, on rational grounds, they ought to switch to a different answer. In addition, this overall tendency can be modified in a coherent manner. The epigram to Chapter 1 describes more precisely what I have tried to do.

PART ONE

Assumptions, Correspondence, and a Look at Initial Monty Hall Studies

CHAPTER 1

MARILYN AND THE THREE DOORS

In any field, find the strangest thing and then explore it.
John Archibald Wheeler (1992)

In the September 9, 1990, issue of **PARADE**, this query was posed to columnist Marilyn vos Savant:

> Suppose you're on a game show and you're given the choice of three doors: Behind one door is a car; behind the others, goats. You pick a door, say No. 1, and the host, who knows what's behind the doors, opens another door, say No. 3, which has a goat. He then says to you, "Do you want to pick door No. 2?" Is it to your advantage to switch your choice?
> —Craig F. Whitaker, Columbia, Md.

Vos Savant's answer was direct and unambiguous:

> Yes; you should switch. The first door has a one-third chance of winning, but the second door has a two-thirds chance. Here's a good way to visualize what happened. Suppose there are a million

doors, and you pick door No. 1. Then the host, who knows what's behind the doors and will always avoid the one with the prize, opens them all except door #777,777. You'd switch to that door pretty fast, wouldn't you?[1]

To say the least, vos Savant's answer was puzzling and counter-intuitive to many, if not most, of her readers. The response she received from the public was massive and overwhelmingly negative. She received more mail on this one problem than on any of her other columns. Many of the people who wrote letters to her concerning her answer were incredulous and irate. This became even more heated when she refused to "recant" and held her ground against her critics in three subsequent columns on the subject.[2]

My position is that her answer was essentially correct. There is a highly plausible set of circumstances under which her answer is valid. Furthermore, her 2/3 solution is the only way that the problem becomes truly interesting. The problem would be entirely trivial and mundane if the answer were simply 1/2, as most of her critics maintained. Anyone who claims that the correct answer must be 50:50 is flat-out wrong.

However, it is difficult to state word problems in an unambiguous way, and there were, as we shall see, real ambiguities in the wording of the problem as it was posed in Marilyn's column. In this opening chapter, I specify the assumptions that are necessary in order for Marilyn's answer to be correct. The reader can then judge whether they stretch things beyond the limit or are, as I maintain, highly reasonable. Then I want to show some of the ways the problem is solved under these assumptions. Finally, we consider some alternative wording that may be less ambiguous.

When the crucial assumptions are made, we have the essential features of this problem which has been called the Standard Monty Hall Dilemma. The name, Monty Hall, is taken from the host of a popular TV show. It aired on U.S. network television for 28 years under the name, "Let's Make

---

1 Marilyn vos Savant, "Ask Marilyn," **PARADE**, September 9, 1990, p. 13.

2 To save people the trouble of locating the microfilms of **PARADE**, I am including all four of Marilyn's columns on the Monty Hall problem as Appendix A.

a Deal."[3] What follows are the crucial assumptions that must be made in order for Marilyn's answer (switch and win with a probability of 2/3) to be correct.

A. **The car is placed randomly with each door having an equal chance.** This information is not given in the question. However, absent any indication to the contrary, it may be the most reasonable assumption to make concerning the location of the prize.

B. **The host knows where the car is and also knows what door the contestant selected initially.** In other words, the host must be knowledge-able in two important respects. It would, of course, be possible for the host to know either fact without necessarily knowing the other. The question stated explicitly that the host "knows what's behind the doors." We are left to assume that the host is also cognizant of the contestant's pick of door No. 1.

C. **The host uses that knowledge to select an unchosen door with a goat to show to the contestant after the contestant's initial guess.** This assumption is necessary because it would be possible, though perhaps not likely, that the host would be knowledgeable and yet select the door to open randomly. So the host must not only be knowledgeable but must also use that knowledge in the way that is specified. This assumption is not made explicit in the wording of the query published in Marilyn's column, but it seems entirely plausible to suppose that a knowledgeable host would use that knowledge.

D. **The host is committed to the procedure of showing an incor-rect, unchosen door after the contestant's initial guess.** Some people have claimed that the host must "always" do this or that. However, if I am the contestant, it really doesn't concern me what the host does in other instances. If I am assured that the host is committed to using this proce-dure with me, that's good enough. In other words, the host cannot have discretion to follow this procedure or some other, based on such things as whether he likes me or which door I selected as my initial guess.

---

3 Monty Hall & Bill Libby, **Emcee Monty Hall**, 1973, New York: Grosset and Dunlap.

E. **If the host has a choice between which of two doors to show, i.e., when the contestant's initial guess is correct, the host's choice is made randomly with equal probability.** Once again, this assumption is not made explicit, but it does seem reasonable enough in the absence of any indication to the contrary. In fact, the wording, "say No. 1" and "say No. 3," should have made it clear that these were just examples of how the game could proceed. Some people have jumped on the example to conclude that the problem, as stated, involves a host who will always prefer to open door 3 if it is incorrect and unchosen. If that were true, the problem would change and become more complex, but I think that is an unreasonable and perhaps even disingenuous reading of the problem.[4]

F. **The host is committed to giving the contestant the choice of whether to stick or switch.** As the problem was stated in Marilyn's column, we don't know on what basis the host decided to offer the chance to switch or stick. Perhaps he only makes that offer when the contestant's initial guess is correct or incorrect, or by some other more complex formula. Her 2/3 solution requires a situation in which the host does not have discretion about whether to make the offer to switch. This is a crucial assumption about which there is real ambiguity in the wording of the question.

G. **The host never lies.** If not for this assumption, the contestant might have some basis for suspecting the whole thing to be a trick. The prize might possibly be moved surreptitiously, depending upon the contestant's initial choice and whether she decides to stick or switch.

Despite the ambiguities, vos Savant deserves a lot of credit for bringing this problem to the public in a stimulating and provocative way. Judging from the massive mail she received, there can be little doubt that she caused large numbers of people to scratch their heads and ponder this problem. I should also add that most people who wrote disagreeing with her answer did not do so over any alleged ambiguity. The overwhelming majority of people who wrote letters dissenting from Marilyn's solution objected for other invalid reasons and was, therefore, simply wrong.

---

4 J.P. Morgan et al., "Let's Make a Deal: The Player's Dilemma," **American Statistician**, 1991, **45**, No .4, 284-287.

Yet it is evident that there were some significant ambiguities in the query which Marilyn answered. One might suppose that was due to the contents of the letter that she received as an inquiry from Mr. Whitaker, which she then published in an unedited form. However, that is not the case. Here is the letter in full, as it was sent from Mr. Whitaker, an actuarial scientist: (Note also the nearly two years between Whitaker's letter and Marilyn's first column on the subject implying no rush to publish.)

November 17, 1988

Ask Marilyn
PARADE
750 Third Avenue
New York, New York 10017

Dear Ms. Savant,

I have enjoyed your puzzles since they first started appearing in PARADE magazine. You seem to be getting less space, sorry to see that.

My puzzle is: Suppose you're on Monty Hall's Let's Make a Deal! You are given the choice of three doors, behind one is a car, the other goats.

You pick a door, say #1, Monty opens another door, say #3, which has a goat. Monty says to you, 'Do you want to pick door #2?' Is it to your advantage to switch your choice of doors?

I've worked out two different situations based upon Monty's prior behavior, (i.e., whether or not he knows what's behind the doors); in one situation it is to your advantage to switch, in the other there is no advantage to switch.

What do you think?
Looking forward to hearing from you,
Craig F. Whitaker
Columbia, MD 21044[5]

---

5 C. Whitaker provided a copy of the letter he sent to Marilyn vos Savant.

The point is that there was considerable editing that was done from the letter as submitted to the published version. Since Marilyn apparently felt free to edit the problem as it was sent to her, she could have eliminated much, if not all, of the ambiguity through more judicious editing. She evidently chose to impose some assumptions in her answer, but it would have been preferable to embed the assumptions in the question.

Various Ways of Solving the Standard Monty Hall Dilemma

Let us for now agree that the above seven assumptions are in place and proceed to various ways that people have used to derive the correct solution. It should be emphasized at the outset that different paths to the solution seem to work best for different people. Having observed this, it is difficult to know just where to begin when other people challenge me to show them a proof of the switch and win with a 2/3 probability solution. Give them five different modes of reasoning, and one may click especially well, but it is hard to know in advance which one that is.

Reasoning Logically. With two losing doors and one winning door, a **knowledgeable** host can always show one losing unchosen door, regardless of which door is chosen initially by the contestant. Thus, when the host **knowingly** opens an incorrect, unchosen door, this gives no additional information about the likelihood of the initially chosen door being the winner. So under these assumptions, the probability of the initially chosen door being correct remains unchanged at 1/3. The probability that one of the unchosen doors contained the prize was 2/3, and that also remains unchanged when the host knowingly opens one of the unchosen doors to show that it is a loser. In effect, the host is offering a choice between the initially chosen door and the other two.

One way of visualizing this line of thinking is by using elementary set theory. In the Standard form of the Monty Hall Dilemma, with all the necessary assumptions being made, the host has, in effect, created two subsets. Initially, the three doors were undifferentiated (Set A). Then when the contestant selects a door, that door is in Subset B, and the other two doors are in Subset C. The probabilities that Subsets B and C contain the prize are 1/3 and 2/3, respectively. No matter what the location of the prize, the knowledgeable host can deliberately show that one of the doors in Subset C is a loser. Under these circumstances, the probability for the door in Subset B remains at 1/3, and the probability for the unopened door in Subset C is 2/3.

This can be further illustrated by the following rewording of the dilemma, done in a way that has the same structure and probabilities. Now it is worded to make the switch and win with 2/3 probability solution more obvious. In this wording, the illusory aspects of this cognitive problem tend to disappear.

> Suppose you are on a game show. The host, who is known to be completely honest, has placed a new car behind one of three doors. "First you point to a door." he says. "Then, regardless of which door you picked, I will give you a choice of staying with that selection and winning whatever is behind that door, or you can trade that door in for the contents of the other two doors." You pick a door, say No. 1, and the host then gives you a choice of staying with door 1 or trading it in for the contents of what is behind both of the other doors 2 and 3. Under these conditions, would you stay with door 1 or switch so you could obtain the contents of both doors 2 and 3?

In an experiment I did, 81% (63/78) of the undergraduate college students randomly assigned to the Standard Monty Hall wording indicated they thought they would stick. This is compared to only 48% (37/77) in the deconstructed version in the preceding paragraph. This difference of 33 percentage points is highly significant.[6]

With the circumstances in the deconstructed version, it doesn't matter if the host knows which door is the winner, since this procedure does not require the host to knowingly open an unchosen, incorrect door. It is assumed that the contestant initially has no basis for differentiating the

---

6 Others may note that it is of interest that only slightly more than half (52%) decided to switch in the deconstructed version. That can be taken as testimony to the "stickiness" of human decisions.

doors on the basis of the likelihood that they contain the prize. But if she did, the rational strategy would be for her to choose the one thought to be least likely to be the winner and then switch away from it. This structure, while it is more transparent, is logically equivalent to the Standard Monty Hall Dilemma. Of course, the whole procedure could be streamlined even farther by having the host inform the contestant, "You may choose any one door or any two doors. What will it be?" The answer then would be easy and simple, but that situation is much less interesting psychologically than the Standard Monty Hall Dilemma.

Enumeration of the Possible Alternatives. A second way of deriving the correct solution to the Standard Monty Hall Dilemma is through an enumeration of all the possibilities. This was one of the favorite techniques of the letter writers, perhaps in part because vos Savant herself used this mode of demonstration in her second column on the Monty Hall Dilemma. Table 1.1 enumerates the possible outcomes when the prize is behind Door A.

Table 1.1

Enumeration of the Possible Sequences in the Monty Hall Dilemma When the Prize is Behind Door A

Contestant chooses door	Host shows door	Contestant switches to door	Win or lose	Probability of this sequence
A	B	C	Lose	1/6
A	C	B	Lose	1/6
B	C	A	Win	1/3
C	B	A	Win	1/3

Contestant chooses door	Host shows door	Contestant sticks with door	Win or Lose	Probability of this sequence
A	B	A	Win	1/6
A	C	A	Win	1/6
B	C	B	Lose	1/3
C	B	C	Lose	1/3

When the contestant selects Door A initially, and the prize is behind it, the host can open either Door B or Door C since either one meets the criteria of being a loser and being unchosen. However, if we assume the placement of the prize is random and the contestant's initial pick is random, Door A would only be correct one-third of the time, and would be the choice in the first stage only one-third of the time.

Therefore, we must divide the probability associated with that outcome in half, as shown in the right-hand column of Table 1.1. A very common error among the letter writers was to enumerate the possibilities in Table 1.1 correctly but then to assign an equal probability of 1/4 to each of the four outcomes. That would require the contestant to choose the correct answer initially with a probability of 1/2 instead of the more probable 1/3.

Table 1.1 assumes that when opening a door, the host knowingly avoids the contestant's initial choice and the prize. It is evident in Table 1.1 that a contestant wins 1/3 of the time by sticking and 2/3 of the time by switching. The enumeration in Table 1.1 would be complete if one added the 16 possibilities that could occur when Door B and Door C contain the prize, but it would be redundant to show this.

Using a Decision Tree. An alternative way to visualize the enumeration of the various possible outcomes and their associated probabilities is through the use of a decision tree.[7] Tree diagrams can show all of the possible outcomes. When one follows the always stick strategy, one wins only when one's initial guess happens to be correct. Of course, that occurs one-third of the times. When one follows the always switch strategy, one wins whenever one's initial guess is incorrect. That happens in two-thirds of the cases. For example, when A contains the winning prize, the contestant wins by choosing B or C initially and then switching to Door A.

Conditional Probability. The correct solution (i.e., switch in the Standard Monty Hall Dilemma) can also be derived by applying the Bayesian formula for conditional probability. If the contestant chooses

---

7 J.M. Shaughnessy & T. Dick, "Monty's: Dilemma: Should you stick or switch?" **Mathematics Teacher**, 1991, **84**, No. 4, 252-256. These math professors at Oregon State University made effective use of decision trees and simulation in their analysis.

Door A and the host opens Door C, what is the probability of Door B containing the prize? The answer, 2/3, can be found by plugging in the right numbers in the following formula, and then solving the equation:

$$P(B|c) = \frac{P(c|B)\ P(B)}{P(c|A)\ P(A) + P(c|B)\ P(B) + P(c|C)\ P(C)}$$

That looks like a rather forbidding formula, but it is really not all that difficult when it is broken down into components. Begin with the assumption that initially the three doors are equally likely to contain the prize: $P(A)=P(B)=P(C)=1/3$. So wherever one of these probabilities, $P(A)$, $P(B)$, or $P(C)$, appears in the formula, substitute 1/3. Next we start with the obvious, what is the probability of c being opened by the host if C is the winner, $P(c|C)$? The answer is that, by the rules, there is no chance. Thus, insert a zero there. Next, what is the chance of c being opened if A is the winner, $P(c|A)$? In that case, the host could open either Door B or Door C, so the answer is 1/2. Finally, what is the probability of c being opened if B is the winner (recall the contestant chose Door A in this example)? The answer is that under those circumstances, the host has no choice but to choose C to disclose, since it is the only incorrect, unchosen alternative. So for $P(c|B)$ in the formula, substitute 1. Now we are ready to plug in the values in the formula to get the probability of Door B containing the winner, given that the contestant picked Door A initially and the host opened Door C, $P(B|c)$.

$$P(B|c) = \frac{(1)(1/3)}{(1/2)(1/3) + (1)(1/3) + (0)(1/3)} = \frac{1/3}{1/2} = \frac{2}{3}$$

The conditional probability of Door A containing the prize if the contestant chooses A initially and the host opens Door C, $P(A|c)$ is derived in the same manner. The denominator remains exactly the same, but the numerator is changed to $P(c|A)\ P(A)$, which is equal to (1/2) (1/3). Thus, the numerator would equal 1/6, and dividing that by the denominator of 1/2 gives the probability of 1/3. That is the conditional probability of winning by sticking in the Standard Monty Hall Dilemma.[8]

Simulation. As you can see, the 2/3 solution can be derived in a variety of ways, from the more verbal to the more mathematical. It can also be demonstrated by a simulation. In her third column, Marilyn suggested students, at whatever level, do a simulation by hand, using nothing more complicated than a die, three paper cups, and a penny, and send her the results. She then printed some of the results in her fourth Monty column. It is quite impressive that many students reported results that confirmed her answer despite their being very doubtful initially.

Others recognized that the dilemma could be simulated via a simple program in which the computer's capacity to generate random numbers was used to run a large number of trials. Gregory Johnson wrote such a program for me at a time when I was still much less than certain. In our simulation, we ran 100 trials of 50, using the always switch strategy. The result was an average of 32.3 wins and a standard deviation of 3.40. For comparison we also ran 100 trials of 50 with the always stick strategy. In this case, the average number of wins was 16.7 with a standard deviation of 3.20. It is well to note that while the results are consistent with the 2/3 win if one always switches, there is quite a lot of variance when the sample consists of 100 runs of 50 trials. When one runs 50 trials, the results will be centered near 17 correct if one always sticks and near 33 correct if one always switches. Note also that there is a slight overlap in the results for the two strategies. The computer simulations have since been run with a million trials, and the results support the strategy of switch and win on 2/3 of the trials.

The Monty Hall Dilemma in Review

Although the Monty Hall Dilemma received a great deal of publicity because of its appearance in Marilyn vos Savant's column in September

---

8 See R. Falk, "A Closer Look at the Probabilities of the Notorious Three Prisoners," **Cognition**, 1992, **43**, No. 3, 197-223.

of 1990, this was not its origin. So far as I can tell, it first appeared in print as a letter to the editor in the February 1975 issue of **American Statistician** written by Steve Selvin, a biostatistician at the University of California at Berkeley. The headline was innocent enough, "A Problem in Probability."

In August of that same year, Selvin had another letter published in the same journal, entitled "On the Monty Hall Problem." In it he cited a general formula credited to D.L. Ferguson, and he also mentioned that Benjamin King pointed out the "critical assumptions" that must be made to solve the problem. In part because it was the first published version and, in part, because some authors have failed to cite Selvin's contribution, e.g., Morgan et al., I decided to reprint, with permission of the author and the journal, Selvin's two brief letters as Appendix B for this book.

Barry Nalebuff published the Monty Hall Dilemma as a puzzle for readers of **Economic Perspectives** in 1987. Solomon Golomb published a fascinating presentation of the Monty Hall Dilemma in 1989 in the **Johns Hopkins Magazine**. It was not until 1995 that behavioral scientists began publishing on the Monty Hall Dilemma. The most intensive and mathematically sophisticated treatment of the Monty Dilemma is provided by Jason Rosenhouse.[9]

On July 21, 1991, the **New York Times** carried an insightful (page 1) article by John Tierney on the Monty Hall Dilemma. In preparing this article, he consulted with Marilyn vos Savant, Persi Diaconis, a Harvard University statistician, and Monty Hall himself! Tierney also gave a version of the problem which does a fine job of embedding the main assumptions discussed earlier. My only quibble is to wonder why Tierney included the motivational level, indicating the contestant wants the car badly. Since it is desirable to streamline word problems whenever possible, that sentence could well be deleted. The dilemma can be real when very much or relatively little is at stake. Nevertheless, it is fitting to end this first chapter with Tierney's wording of the Standard Monty Hall Dilemma:

---

9 J. Rosenhouse, **The Monty Hall Problem: The Remarkable Story of Math's Most Contentious Brainteaser**, 2009, New York: Oxford University Press.

Monty Hall, a thoroughly honest game-show host, has placed a car behind one of three doors. There is a goat behind each of the other doors. "First you point to a door," he says. "Then I'll open one of the other doors to reveal a goat. After I've shown you the goat, you make your final choice, and you win whatever is behind that door."

You want the car very badly. You point to a door. Mr. Hall opens another door to show you a goat. There are two closed doors remaining, and you have to make your decision: Should you stick with the door you chose? Or should you switch to the other door? Or doesn't it matter?

CHAPTER 2

SOME CLOSE COUSINS: PROBLEMS RELATED TO THE MONTY HALL DILEMMA

Among academics, there has been a long standing interest in visual or optical illusions.[1] This was related to the venerable philosophical concern over the relationship between mind and matter. Psychophysics, the focus in the early days of experimental psychology, related changes in the physical world to changes in the psychological realm.

For example, if we gradually increase the brightness of a light, sooner or later it will register as a change in the psychological experience of a normal person. Perhaps the most famous, and easiest to demonstrate, visual illusion is the Müller-Lyer illusion in which one line with feathers pointing outward appears to be longer than a line of equal length in which the arrow fins are pointing inward. As another example, consider the top hat illusion in which a vertical line is seen as longer than the horizontal line. See Figure 2.1. Such tendencies are strong enough and reliable enough to

---

1 E.G. Boring, **Sensation and Perception in the History of Experimental Psychology**, 1942, New York: Appleton-Century.

justify raising the evolutionary question of whether such illusions facilitate adaptation to the environment.

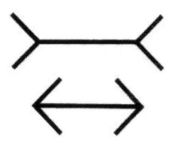

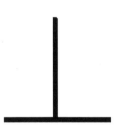

Figure 2.1 Two Common Optical Illusions, the Müller Lyer Illusion (above) and the Horizontal-Vertical (top hat) Illusion (below)

The Monty Hall Dilemma can be regarded as a **cognitive illusion** in that the actual probabilities are substantially different from what they **seem** to be. Similarly, in the long run, we may wish to know if susceptibility to the Monty Hall Dilemma is, in any discernible way, adaptive for individuals or for a culture.

In the past 25 years, attention has turned to whether people are good naïve statisticians. The jury is still out on such matters, but some very clear examples abound where the intuitions people have about statistics and probabilities are misleading and erroneous. A few examples of these cognitive illusions will serve to illustrate the point.

A. Do boys have more sisters, on average, than brothers?
B. Do girls have more brothers, on average, than sisters?
C. Do boys have more sisters than girls have sisters?
D. Do girls have more brothers than boys have brothers?

If you think about this for a minute or two, the answers may seem self-evident. Think, for instance, of a two-child family with one boy and one girl. In that family, the boy will have one sister and no brothers; the girl will have one brother and no sisters. Or consider a family with four children, two boys and two girls. In such a family, each boy will have one brother and two sisters; each girl will have one sister and two brothers. It seems obvious that the answer to each of the four questions beginning this paragraph is yes. Yet what seems to be so true turns out not to be true at all!

When I heard about this problem and considered it on logical grounds, my strong inclination as an empirically oriented social scientist was to get some relevant data. It turns out that, in reality, girls and boys have approximately equal number of brothers and sisters. When this question was posed by Ruma Falk to Marilyn vos Savant, Marilyn's correct response contained this explanation:

> Strange as it may seem, men and women have an equal number of sisters and brothers. This is because repeatedly choosing at random one child from a family and noting how many sisters and/or brothers he or she has amounts to randomly removing one child from all families and simply counting the females and males left. Assuming an even male/female distribution of the sexes, these numbers will be about the same.[2]

---

2 M. vos Savant and R. Falk, **The Power of Logical Thinking**, 1996, New York: St. Martin's, pp.26-29.

As a second example where the intuitive statistician goes astray, consider the birthday problem. This problem is strictly a matter of probability and is found in many basic textbooks on statistics and probability. Start with an empty room, and have randomly chosen people enter one at a time. How many people must enter before the probability reaches .5 that at least two people in the room have the same birthday? For many people, the intuitive answer is 365/2 or about 182. When I asked college students to guess the answer, the average estimate was about 184, far in excess of the correct answer (23).[3] Overall, 88% (50/57) of the students gave guesses larger than 23. This is a cognitive illusion.

Nor is it only amateurs who have a difficult time when trying their hands at intuitive statistics. Gottfried Wilhelm von Leibniz, who achieved great fame as the co-founder of calculus, once opined that one is just as likely to roll a 12 as one is to roll 11 in a throw of two dice. In fact, a roll of 11 is twice as likely as a roll of 12 (1/18 compared to 1/36).[4]

In a similar vein, consider the following passage in a recent book, **My Brain is Open**, a biography of Paul Erdős.[5]

> On Erdős's last visit with his old friend, Andrew Vázsonyi, Vázsonyi . . . decided to test Erdős's probabilistic intuition with the . . . Monty Hall problem. . . . Erdős was one the world's leading authorities on probability. Vázsonyi expected that Erdős would immediately penetrate to the heart of the Monty Hall problem as he had with many far more difficult problems.
>
> Vázsonyi told Erdős that the correct strategy was to switch, "and I fully expected to move on to the next subject. But Erdős,

---

3 H. Alder and E. Roessler, **Introduction to Probability and Statistics**, 1968 (4th ed.), San Francisco: Freeman. The solution is 1 x 364/365 x 363/365 x 362/365 x . . . 343/365 = .493 and 1 − .493=.507 which is the probability that in a group of 23 people, at least two of them will have the same birthday.

4 M. Gardner, "Mathematical games: Problems involving questions of probability and ambiguity," **Scientific American**, 1959, **201**, No. 4, 174-182. There are two ways an 11 can occur and only one way a 12 can occur.

5 B. Schechter, **My Brain is Open: The Mathematical Journeys of Paul Erdős**, 1998, New York: Simon and Schuster, pp.107-109.

to my surprise, said, 'No, that is impossible, it should make no difference. . . .'" Eventually, frustrated by Vázsonyi's explanations, Erdős stormed away. When Erdős returned an hour later he shouted at Vázsonyi, "You are not telling me why to switch! What is the matter with you?" Erdős became convinced of the wisdom of that course of action only after Vázsonyi showed him a simulation on his computer, but he still was frustrated by his inability to understand intuitively why switching worked. Erdős was finally mollified a few days later after . . . Ron Graham, a mathematician at Bell Labs explained the problem to his satisfaction (pp. 107-109).

Similarly, I described the Monty Hall Dilemma to my good friend and math whiz, Erv Dotseth. After thinking about it for a minute or two, Erv said, "It sounds like a 50-50 proposition to me." He later came around and even used the Monty Hall Dilemma in some lectures he gave.

Given that these exceptional figures had trouble with the probabilities in the Monty Hall Dilemma, we turn now to a consideration of some situations that resemble in some important ways the Monty Hall Dilemma. The purpose is to advance understanding of the Monty Hall Dilemma and to ponder whether it is unique in some important way.

Bertrand's Box Paradox

In his book, *Calcul des Probabilités* (1888), Joseph Bertrand, the great French mathematician, posed a problem now known as Bertrand's Box Paradox: Consider a chest of drawers that has three drawers. In one drawer (A) are two silver coins. In another drawer (B) are one silver coin and one gold coin, and in a third drawer (C) there are two gold coins. A drawer is drawn at random, and from that drawer a coin is drawn at random. The coin drawn is gold. What then is the probability that it is from the drawer C?

Here the intuitive answer is 1/2, but this is wrong. The correct answer is 2/3. After the drawing, we know that it cannot be from drawer A since A did not contain any gold coin. Therefore, there are three possibilities as to the source of the gold coin. The gold coin could be the one gold coin in drawer B, gold coin c-1 from drawer C or gold coin c-2 from drawer C. Therefore, the conditional probability is 2/3. When the 1/2 and 2/3 probabilities occur together, these familiar probabilities may cause one to suspect that the problem resembles the Monty Hall Dilemma. Indeed it does in certain respects, but as we shall see later, there is still something unique about the Monty Hall Dilemma.

An analogous problem concerns the gender of a parent's two children. If a parent says, "One of my children is a boy, what is the likelihood that both of them are boys?" Assuming that he has chosen by some random process the child whose gender he has revealed, then the probability is only 1/3 that both of his children are boys. This is shown by considering the permutations that could occur. Before he says anything, the four possibilities are two boys (BB), one boy and one girl (BG and GB), and two girls (GG). When the man reveals that one of the children is a boy, the only possibility that is eliminated is GG. With the other three possibilities each having an equal chance, the probability of two boys is only 1/3. On the other hand, if the man had randomly chosen one child to describe more specifically, e.g., "My oldest child is a boy. What is the probability that both of my children are boys?" Then there are two possibilities that are eliminated (GG and GB) so there are two remaining possibilities, BG and BB. Each of the latter possibilities has a 1/2 chance of being true. So in that case, the probability of both of the parent's children being boys is 1/2.[6]

The Three Prisoner Problem

What we now call the three prisoner problem was introduced in 1959 by Martin Gardner.[7] For many years, Gardner wrote the Mathematical Games section of the **Scientific American**. Six years later, Frederick Mostellar included an alternative version of the three prisoner problem in

---

6 R. Falk, "A closer look at the probabilities of the notorious three prisoners," **Cognition**, 1992, **43**, No. 3, 197-223.

7 M. Gardner, op. cit.

his **Fifty Challenging Problems in Probability**.[8] Gardner's original for-mulation is truncated here as follows:

Three prisoners, Tom, Dick, and Harry, were each scheduled to be executed on a given date. Moved by mercy, the Governor decided to par-don one of them. He decided, by some arbitrary method, e.g., a single roll of a die, which man would be pardoned. The Governor told no one except for the Warden. For a time, the Warden kept his pledge of secrecy. However, one day Dick approached the Warden, and made this proposal, "I understand that you can't tell me if I am to get a pardon. But could you please tell me the name of one of the other two convicts who is to be executed? If Tom is to be pardoned you could name Harry as one who is to be executed. If Harry is to be pardoned, name Tom as one who is to be executed. If I am to receive the pardon, decide by some random method whether to name Harry or Tom as one who is to be executed." The Warden reasons that he would follow a comparable procedure if requested to do so by one of the other inmates. Therefore, he tells Dick, "Tom is to be executed." Dick is happy because he thinks the probability of his getting a pardon has increased from 1/3 to 1/2. Is Dick justified in his belief? Can we say anything about Harry's prospects?[9]

In Mosteller's version, there are two good outcomes and one bad out-come, while in Gardner's, delineated above, there are one good and two bad outcomes. (This difference becomes important to us when we get to Chapter 6.)

The Two Envelope Problem

Barney Bissinger of Hershey, Pennsylvania, posed this dilemma in another of Marilyn vos Savant's columns, this one from September 20,

---

8 F. Mosteller, **Fifty Challenging Problems in Probability with Solutions**, 1965, Reading, MA: Addison Wesley.

9 M. Gardner, "Mathematical games: How three mathematicians disproved a celebrated con-jecture of Leonard Euler," **Scientific American**, 1959, **201**, No. 5, 181-188. There appears to be an error in Gardner's text. In the first part, he writes that prisoner B was going to be executed. But in the second part, he states that B's chances of being pardoned are 2/3. I have substituted C for B as the prisoner whose chances of being pardoned are 2/3. With that change, the problem makes sense.

1992, slightly more than a year after her fourth and final column on the Monty Hall Dilemma.

> I am asked to select one of two envelopes and told only that one contains twice as much money as the other. I find $100 in the envelope I select. Should I switch to the other one to improve my worldly gains?

Marilyn's answer:

> This is a dandy paradox. While it appears as though you should switch, because you have an even chance for $200 vs. $50—which any gambler would grab—it actually makes no difference at all. Those even chances would apply only if you could choose one of two **more** envelopes, one with $200 and the other with $50.
>
> As it is, there's just one more envelope sitting there, with either twice the amount you've already seen or half of it. And you knew that would be the case before you even started. So, when you opened the first envelope, you didn't gain any information to improve your chances. This can be illustrated by noting that the logic that causes you to switch (because you appear to have an even chance for $200 vs. $50) will lead you to switch every time (no matter what you find in the first envelope), making the second envelope just as randomly chosen as the first one![10]

The problem had been presented in a similar form by Professors J. Michael Shaughnessy and Thomas Dick in the February, 1992 issue of **Mathematics Teacher**.[11] This two envelope problem can be analyzed, albeit inappropriately, by considering the expected value. For sticking with the envelope you've chosen and seen, the "expected value" is $100. For switching the "expected value" is [(200 + 50)/2] = $125. So it would appear

---

10 M. vos Savant, "Ask Marilyn," **PARADE**, September 20, 1992, p.20.

11 J. Shaughnessy and T. Dick, "Monty's revenge," **Mathematics Teacher**, 1992, **85**, No. 2, 91.

that one should switch. However, no such general solution is viable. In this case, the judgment must take into account the context, namely, what is a reasonable prior condition to expect given the setting? If one is in a typical psychology experiment, even the $100 would likely be viewed as implausibly large. Conditioning our choice on this basis, it is unlikely that one could gain by switching. On the other hand, if one were on a prime time television show, the $100 or $200 would be entirely plausible and perhaps at the low end of possible expected payoffs. Therefore, it might be altogether reasonable to switch in one context but not in another.

The Waiting Game

The waiting game deals with the amount of time or the number of events one can expect to occur before some designated event occurs. It was first depicted in 1969 in a brief note by W. Penney.[12] It can be illustrated by considering any dichotomy such as heads vs. tails, boy vs. girl, or black vs. white. Assume that the alternatives in the dichotomy are equally likely. Then say we choose in sequence three children. There are then eight possibilities where B=Boy and G=Girl: BBB, BBG, BGB, BGG, GGB, GBG, GBB, and GGG. In a random draw from the beginning, i.e., "starting from scratch," these eight alternatives are equally likely, each having a probability of 1/8.

However, if we continue the draw until a certain designated triplet is observed, the expected waiting times for the various permutations are **not** equal. Waiting time in this context refers to the number of events, on average, that would be expected to occur prior to, and including, the occurrence of the designated triplet. For example, the waiting time for the triplet GGG is 14. This means the number of instances of the draw needed for this triplet to occur would be a distribution centered at 14. Expected waiting times are symmetrical in that the average waiting time for the triplet BBB is also 14.

---

12 W. Penney, "A waiting time problem," **Journal of Recreational Mathematics**, 1969, **2**, No. 4, 241.

Penney's editor, David Silverman, referred to this problem as "completely unintuitive."[13] Gardner, in one of his **Scientific American** columns in 1974 referred to this problem as "one of the most incredible of all non-transitive betting situations."[14] He added, "It is not well known, and most mathematicians simply cannot believe it when they hear of it. It is certainly one of the finest of all sucker bets." (Here non-transitive means that if A is greater than B, and B is greater than C, it does not necessarily follow that A is greater than C.)

The average waiting times for the eight triplets are 8 for BBG, BGG, GBB, and GGB; 10 for BGB and GBG, and 14 for BBB and GGG. Now we come to the most amazing aspect of this situation. Suppose you have two players, choosing triplets in sequence. One person picks one of the eight triplets. The other person chooses one of the remaining seven triplets. Then a random letter generator selects a string of letters, continuing until one of the chosen triplets occurs. The person whose chosen triplet occurs first wins that trial. If play is limited to one round, the person choosing second can always gain an advantage in picking the alternative likely to show up first, i.e., the triplet with the shortest waiting time. Gardner's 1974 article shows that no matter which triplet person one chooses first, there is one alternative that clearly stacks the odds in favor of person two choosing last. The advantage of choosing last is at least 2:1, but ranges up to 7:1. Thus, the person choosing last has the favorable situation, and there is a specific triplet that will provide the best odds.

One could say that this problem is an instance where it pays to "get the last word in." The rational player will always endeavor to choose last and will always switch. An endless round of choices could occur if rival rational players are always given the opportunity to switch in light of their opponent's most recent choice.

Since we are getting started we might suggest limiting the number of decisions. For example, it could be limited to two decisions for player one.

---

13 D. Silverman, "Blind penny-ante," **Journal of Recreational Mathematics**, 1969, **2**, No. 4, 241.

14 M. Gardner, "Mathematical games: On the paradoxical situations that arise from non-transitive relations," **Scientific American**, 1974, **231**, No. 4, 120-125.

Player one picks one of the triplets. Player two, a shill, picks the rational (correct) alternative. Then player one is given the opportunity to switch. The important question is not only does player one switch, but also does player one switch to the single best, i.e., optimal alternative. In another condition, only two choices would be made. Player one is the shill and chooses randomly with the limitation that on every eight trials, each option would be used just once. Then player two makes a countering choice, and the question is whether the countering choice is the optimal one, given player one's selection on that trial.

Resemblance to the Monty Hall Dilemma

We have introduced four games that bear some resemblance to the Monty Hall Dilemma. Bertrand's Box, along with some variants regarding the gender of a parent's children, alerts us to the fact that calculating probabilities can be a tricky business. However, these problems are not isomorphic to the Monty Hall Dilemma. They do not involve any two-stage decisions which is what makes the Monty Hall Dilemma so excruciating and yet delightful.

Much the same can be said for the three prisoner's problem. The warden plays about the same role as the host in the Monty Hall Dilemma. Therefore, the warden is a source of information, but he must not play favorites. That is, the warden cannot decide whether to provide the information, based on whether Prisoner A is the one to be pardoned. The apparent effect on A's assessment of his prospects for receiving a pardon seems to be what is at issue in this scene. However, A's fate is not dependent on a guess by A followed by a decision of A to stick or switch. The probabilities are essentially the same for the three prisoner problem as for the Monty Hall Dilemma. In the prisoner problem, prisoner A cannot affect the outcome by using a stick or switch strategy.

The two envelope problem has the stick or switch decision, but here there is no simple or correct strategy. The always switch strategy of the Monty Hall Dilemma does not generalize to the two envelope problem. The only solution to the two envelope problem, other than deciding randomly, would be to consider information about prior and current conditions. In a multiple trial situation, one could look for a departure from randomness in the placement of the larger amount of money.

Of the situations considered here, the waiting game is most similar to the Monty Hall Dilemma. One difference is that in the Monty Hall Dilemma, the crucial relationship is between a host and a contestant. It may, but also may not, take on the character of a zero sum game. The waiting game is a zero sum game between the two players, as they interact in a situation contrived by the experimenter. The waiting game is a rather demanding game in that the naïve statistician is required not only to understand enough to always switch, but also to know which specifically of the remaining options to choose while switching. So far as I know, the waiting game has not been used in any empirical study. The safe prediction is that people will tend to stick when they should switch. Also, it is likely that the only rational aspect naïve subjects will show is that they will avoid the homogeneous triplets (GGG and BBB). It is doubtful that they will identify the advantage of choosing last.

CHAPTER 3
SOME OF MARILYN'S MAIL

A very bright gal named Savant
Made a game show mistake quite flagrant,
Ph.D.'s by the throng
Wrote to tell her she's wrong,
But she wouldn't 'fess up or recant.

William J. Cohagan

As a prelude to the letters to Marilyn, let us briefly review the sequence of events. On September 9, 1990, Marilyn published her first column on the Monty Hall Dilemma. It consisted of the letter from Craig Whitaker, together with her answer in which she sought to advance the switch and win with a 2/3 probability solution. Her answer focused on the metaphor of expanding the number of doors to a million. Her second column on December 2 contained the harsh criticism from three Ph.D.'s (incidentally only one of whom was a mathematician). Marilyn stood her ground, using the 3 shells and a pea game, and a table giving 6 possible outcomes. She encouraged people to play the game with an Ace and 2 Jokers.

In the third column, published on February 17, 1991, Marilyn included excerpts from 10 mostly irate and puzzled readers. She reported the results indicating that 90% of the letter writers disagreed with her switch and win 2/3 of the time solution, including 92% of the general public and 65% of the letters from universities. She also made another defense of her view and then invited math classes around the country to try it out using a penny, 3 cups, and a die. She suggested that they play 400 trials, sticking 200 times and switching 200 times.

Students were requested to tally the results and report them to her. Marilyn's fourth column on July 7, 1991, consisted in the main of letters from teachers and students. Some had performed the experiment exactly as she had suggested, while others wrote a computer simulation. Nearly all who tried the inductive experiment now accepted her 2/3 solution.

In what follows we report a non-random sampling of opinions expressed by the letter writers. In most cases they represent a way of responding that was not unique. We begin with one of the more vociferous letters writers.

> Dear Ms. "vos Savant":
>
> Let me not pull my punches. As a high school math teacher, I must say that your article of Dec. 2, 1990, abundantly demonstrates the impoverished intellectual state of our society at large. Are you so fatuously confident that you are willing to unabashedly challenge, in print, three PhD mathematicians (See Appendix A) on a high school probability problem? My tenth graders can easily solve such problems after a three week introduction to probability in the Algebra II course. Do you have a high school diploma?
>
> What a scam you're running with your column. Perhaps I'll start a column in competition with you; I'll title it "Correct answers to the questions asked of Marilyn 'vos Savant'."
>
> Your entry in the <u>Guinness Book of World Records</u> merely puts you in the company of champion pogo stick jumpers. I challenge you to print your detailed academic credentials, particularly your mathematical credentials, in your next column. Regrettably yours,
>
> Ransome Weis

Writing from the Harvard University Center for Astrophysics, E. Samuel Palmer captured the ambivalent feelings many people may have experienced:

> Dear Marilyn
>
> The responsible side of me was disheartened to read the letters you published in the December 2 Parade, but another side (the real me, no doubt) was delighted. I hope these patronizing gentlemen are suitably embarrassed to find themselves bagged by a very common statistics mistake.
>
> Your column is an example of an effective approach to understanding problems of this kind: Ask the question, get predictions (with or without supporting arguments), then do the experiment. In discussing the results and trying to account for them in statistical terms, people have a much better opportunity to gain some insight. . . .
>
> In choosing a door you divide the doors into two groups. The first group contains one door with a 1/3 chance of hiding the prize and the second group contains two doors which together have a 2/3 chance of hiding the prize. In switching, you choose the second group. In other words, the problem has this equivalent statement: There is a prize behind one of the three doors. You may choose one door, or you may choose any pair of doors. Even the learned PhD's might recognize the latter as the better choice.

A very similar insight occurred to another person at a very different station in life:

> Dear Marilyn:
> As a professional Gambler/Grifter serving a life sentence at Angola, La. I lack Ph.D. credentials. It did however take me 40 seconds to determine you are absolutely correct. . . . To win by not switching,

you must initially make the correct choice, which of course is twice as difficult with only 1 correct choice.
Sincerely,
Kirksey M. Nix, Jr.

Nor does a lofty affiliation assure one of being correct. William Camann of Harvard University's Medical School wrote a letter accusing Marilyn of several errors. In fact, the errors were his. For instance, he made the common error of claiming there were eight outcomes instead of six without realizing that the probabilities for two of the eight would have to be cut in half (see Table 1.1). He was also confused over the difference between odds and probability. Then he falsely accused Marilyn of being inconsistent when she pointed out that the probability of the initially chosen door doesn't go up just because an unchosen losing door is opened. If so, he added, how can the probability of the other unchosen door go up, "Either the odds can change or they can not, but you can't have it both ways. Marilyn, be consistent." But he ended his long letter on a conciliatory note:

> I hope I have adequately explained why your answer to this game show is in error. . . . I do hope that this matter receives further attention in your column because I really believe that your answer is wrong. Remember, even the greatest minds occasionally make a mistake, and one of the hallmarks of greatness is the ability to admit to those mistakes.
>
> I would be happy to discuss the content of this letter with you at greater length if you wish. As a scientist who frequently performs statistical analyses for medical researchers, I would also be pleased to consult with you about any other matters of a statistical or mathematical nature.
> Yours sincerely,
> William Camann, M.D
> Harvard Medical School

By February 19, 1991, Dr. Camann had changed his mind as indicated in this follow-up letter:

> In my previous letter, I attempted to explain at some length and detail why your answer was in error. I openly admit that it was I, not you, who was in error. I congratulate you for sticking to your guns in the face of what must have seemed to be overwhelming opposition to your stance. I always have, and will always continue to be, a faithful reader of your column.
>> Yours sincerely,
>> William Camann
>> Harvard Medical School

A rather typical wrong answer was sent on December 3, 1990, the day after Marilyn's second column appeared:

> Marilyn:
> WRONG AGAIN! Before any of the doors open there are 3 possible outcomes:

	Door 1	Door 2	Door 3
I	AUTO	GOAT	GOAT
II	GOAT	AUTO	GOAT
III	GOAT	GOAT	AUTO

> After door 3 is opened and a goat is revealed, only 2 possible outcomes remain (I and II). Both are equally probable, so that switching does not increase or decrease your chances of winning.
> Karen K. Gleason, Ph.D., M.I.T.

The Angered Letter-Writers

Not all of Marilyn's critics responded so calmly and matter-of-factly as the previous letter. In other letters, Marilyn was called arrogant, blockhead, stubborn, pig-headed, stupid, lacking in common sense, Ms. Smarty Pants, among other pejoratives. Some writers were infuriated by Marilyn's columns, while some swore they would not read her column in the future. Some addressed their concerns to **PARADE** and some writers who disagreed with her about the Monty Hall Problem, called for her to be fired. Here are a few of the many angered letter writers.

> Editorial Office
> Parade Magazine
> Dear Sirs:
> The article by Marilyn vos Savant on page 25 of the December 2 Parade is egregiously incorrect. If you value the reputation of Parade, you would be well advised to publish a disclaimer to the effect that the opinions expressed are her own and not those of the editors of Parade. It is beyond belief that this pathetic attempt to refute her critics could have been written by one with the highest I.Q. on record. The statement that "the winning odds of 1/3 on the first choice can't go up to 1/2 just because the host opens a losing door" is absurd on its face. Like Robert Sachs (quoted in the article) I am concerned about the general public's lack of mathematical skills, and it is most unfortunate that so influential an organ as Parade should propagate erroneous mathematics.
> Thomas Greville, Ph.D.
> Charlottesville, VA

From State College, Pennsylvania came this rather hostile letter:

> Dear Marilyn,
> Anyone is entitled to err once, even twice or thrice, but in your most recent column (December 2, 1990, Parade) you have committed what I consider to be unpardonable sins. It is

distressing to think you could be so conceited as to believe that you were correct when three distinguished scholars took the time to write to you and point out your error. It is inconceivable that you would publicly identify them and bluntly state that they were wrong, based upon a "clarification" which was also incorrect. As an educator, I find your 2 December column reprehensible, and urge you to reconsider your future endeavors. In my opinion, you no longer provide a useful service to your readers. . . .

I believe your 2 December article has discredited your reputation and accordingly, I am encouraging Parade Magazine to drop your column. I also would encourage your publisher to print a strong apology to the three scholars whose wisdom was impugned by your illogical babble. I hope they sue you!

> Most sincerely,
> Gregory S. Forbes

The next letter is of special interest because of the follow up and the lofty credentials:

> September 9, 1990

Dear Marilyn:

Your analysis of the prize behind the door problem (Parade, Sept. 9, 1990) is not correct. In the case of three doors, after the host opens door 3, the chance that the prize is behind door 1 is one-half. In the extension to 1,000,000 doors, after the host opens 999,998 doors, leaving only door 1 and 777,777 closed, the chance that the prize is behind door 1 is also one-half.

The error in your reasoning is quite common, and I shall be glad to explain it to you, if you call me any time at the number listed above.

> Sincerely,
> Paul Slepian

34

Interestingly, Dr. Slepian did not let the matter rest there. Instead, after the publication of Marilyn's second Monty column, he addressed himself in no uncertain terms to the editor of **PARADE** magazine.

Editor:

My mathematics credentials are listed at the end of this letter.[1] In September, Marilyn incorrectly answered a question referring to the probability of a prize behind one of three closed doors. Several professors of mathematics, including me, wrote to her, noting the error. I have, on my shelf, more than 50 probability texts, each of which solves the problem correctly, and warns against Marilyn's error, as a result frequently obtained by unskilled mathematical amateurs.

Today, Marilyn devoted an entire column to the problem, and included some of the critical letters. However, instead of graciously acknowledging her mistake, she ridiculed the comments of the professors, and incredibly persisted with the myopic, convoluted logic which led to her original untenable result. Her defense of a known error today damaged Parade's reputation for the truth. Her column should be discontinued.

Sincerely,
Paul Slepian

Out of curiosity, I wrote to him, sending him the two papers by Steve Selvin from the **American Statistician** among other relevant material. I asked him for 5 or 10 citations out of the 50 he had mentioned in his letter, and I asked him if he had any additional thoughts on the subject that he might want to share with me. He responded by phone, making no mention

---

1   These included S.B., MIT, Ph.D., Brown University, both in mathematics, 40 years of university teaching at Brown University, University of Southern California, University of Arizona, Rensselaer Polytechnic Institute, Bucknell University (Chairman), Howard University. Consultant: Los Alamos Scientific Laboratory, Argonne National Laboratory, Jet Propulsion Laboratory, Sandia Laboratories, Institute for Defense Analyses. Author: More than 30 published research papers and a published graduate text. Credentials listed in Who's Who in America, American Men of Science, etc.

of the 50 textbooks supporting his view, and later sent me this follow-up letter:

> Dear Prof. Granberg:
>
> My telephone conversation with you can be neatly summarized by the following:
>
> Consider a box with 2 black balls and 1 red ball. I am blindfolded and reach in and extract 1 ball. Now, consider the following two cases:
>
> Case 1: A black ball rolls out of the box.
>
> The chance that I have the red ball is one-half.
>
> Case 2: An observer, with no blindfold, looks in and extracts a black ball, deliberately. The chance that
>
> I have the red ball is one third.
>
> I claim that in Marilyn's original presentation, she implied Case 1 only. Later, in her arguments attempting to justify her original answer (which, in Case 1, was wrong), she tried to show that her original presentation was, indeed, Case 2. Unfortunately, she did not distinguish clearly between the two cases.
>
> Sincerely,
>
> Paul Slepian

The preceding three letter-writers were definitely among the group of critics who expressed their feelings most strongly. However, strong feelings were not limited to those who disagreed with Marilyn's 2/3 solution. The following author contributed a 13 page paper which he submitted with this vitriolic letter:

> Dear Ms. vos Savant:
>
> Please find the enclosed paper which contains a proof of the general case of n doors with k empty doors revealed by the host. REAL mathematicians consider this a trivial problem. Your solution is the correct one and any REAL mathematician can produce a proof of its correctness. My first question is: WHAT discipline do these

respondents have their Ph.D.'s in? Is it adolescent behavior? If it is in mathematics, then my second question is: What institution granted it? Really, their behavior is so disgusting I have lost sleep over it.

My undergraduate students have solved this problem for years. I can't believe these "educated" people have attacked you the way they have. It just reinforces that old adage:

YOU CAN BRING AN ASS TO WATER, BUT YOU CAN'T MAKE IT DRINK!

Good luck and good wishes from Massachusetts.
Sincerely,
Stephen J. Turner (Ph.D.....ugh!)

Second Thoughts

It became apparent while reading these letters that some people changed their minds about the Monty Hall problem. This could be evidenced by a person tracing their thought process in a single letter. Also, despite their sticking their necks out and being quoted in Marilyn's second or third column, many of those quoted Ph.D.'s relented and apologized to Marilyn for their impetuous error. Here we consider only a few of the many letter-writers who wrote more than once:

Dear Ms. vos Savant:

Oops. Several days ago I sent a rather long letter detailing why you were wrong about the doggone Game Show problem. A little more reflection on the problem finally led me down the correct path; you are and were, of course, quite right about the answer. Weighted probabilities are apparently a little tricky even for those who should know better. The trick for me was in remembering what you had said in your initial response when you posited the problem with 1,000,000 doors instead of just three. I didn't get it then, but I certainly do now. However, until I drew the analogy between this problem and white and black marbles, I would have bet the farm

that you were wrong. Thank God I don't have a farm and that I have not been on a sufficiently rich reinforcement schedule for gambling to engage in it very often. Thanks also for an interesting column.
Sincerely,
Rick Graber, Ph.D.

The next letters start out with a strongly worded version, but end on a conciliatory note:

Dear Marilyn:

Ignorance and stubbornness are not a good combination; but that is exactly what you seem to display in your analysis of the Auto-Goat problem. . . . The "switching" strategy is no better or no worse than the "staying" strategy. Your "learned opposition" is not so naive after all, and it is rather disappointing that there is nothing exciting for math classes Monday morning.

I think at least two apologies from you are in order: the first to the members of faculty all over the country for the veiled suggestion that they might **need** to consider getting "valid statistics" by actually simulating the game; the second to the student population for any false hopes of "extra credit" your column might have aroused among the gullible—especially at this time of the semester with the final exams just around the corner.
Sincerely,
Appa Rao Korukonda, Ph.D.

Four days later, there came this letter from Saint Bonaventure University marked URGENT:

Dear Marilyn,

Contrary to what I stated in my letter dated December 2, 1990, I think I can now say that it was I who blew it! . . . So there is, after all, something exciting here for Math classes all over the country. Your credibility is no doubt, quite in tact (*sic)* and if any apologies are due, your "learned opposition," myself included, owes you one.

Sincerely,

Appa Rao Korukonda, Ph.D.

From Bartlesville, Oklahoma came this letter:

Dear Marilyn,

I'm afraid I won the goat. Please disregard my previous letter. My two attempts at the game show puzzle proves the difficulty of understanding and applying statistics. I considered that a new game began when the host opened the 3rd door and did not consider the option of opening the 2nd door. Under those conditions, for example, if a new player appeared after one door was open, the chance would be one of two of getting the car. But, the latter assumptions were not the game.

I really did not believe it until we wrote and ran a program. After 10,000 attempts, 6,703 were wins if one changed their choice, pretty close to the expected 2/3rds. It was a good mind teasing puzzle.

Sincerely,

Bernard Baldwin, hat in hand Ph.D.

From Pelican Rapids, Minnesota came this letter expressing second thoughts.

Dear Marilyn,

Please forgive me for my sarcastic remarks in my previous letters concerning the game show problem. You were correct and my students will be so informed. It was my mind that was closed, not yours. How could I have been so foolish? I hope that you will continue to offer similar problems in the future.

With sincere apologies,

Gerald Polley

One of the most puzzling letters came from D.B. She had her students do 775 trials of the version of the Monty Hall problem Marilyn had recommended in her third Monty column. The penny was correctly located on 221 of 333 switch trials (66.4%) and on 180 of 442 stay trials (40.7%). This difference of nearly 26 percentage points is obviously statistically significant. After reporting these results and outlining what she thought the outcome would be, she concluded that you win 50% of the time whether you stick or switch!

Dear Marilyn,

By counting the possible outcomes, the contestant has a 50% chance of winning no matter where the winning door, whether the contestant stays or changes. The United States of America is doing 90% on this test of thinking abilities according to your statistics (evidently a reference to Marilyn's breakdown of the letter writers in her third column). My condolences to the fine staff at MIT (an apparent reference to Seth Kalson, of MIT who was the only supporter of Marilyn's quoted in the third column) and my best wishes for you as you deal with how to admit your error.
Sincerely,
D.B.

Fortunately, the story doesn't end there. A little more than a month later, D.B. sent another letter:

Dear Ms. vos Savant:

Now I must admit to a couple of errors! Please forgive me, but we are learning a lot from these things besides mathematics. I assumed correctly that part of our data was skewed as we all know experimental data can be. I had a nagging little question but no time to identify or worry about it with all the other tasks involved in teaching. . . . I took time to call my most loved teacher at Indiana University, Prof Bill E. Rhoades. He told me I needed to look for something that wasn't clearly stated in your article. Then he sent me a copy of "Monty's Dilemma: Should You Stick or Switch?" by J. Michael Shaughnessy and Thomas Dick in the April 1991 **Mathematics Teacher**. Soon, I had all the conditional probabilities computed and realized the errors.

Sincerely,

D.B.

The Gender Issue

It is difficult to say with any precision how large a factor gender was in generating mail to Marilyn vos Savant on the Monty Hall question. Nevertheless, there are strong hints that it played some role. To begin with, in response to columns 1 and 2, Marilyn included excerpts of the letters from 13 men and no women. Bennett Eisenberg, of the Department of Mathematics at Lehigh University, noticed this and inquired,

> Dear Marilyn,
>
> In reading the letters from people about your solution to the "goat-car" problem I noticed that all were written by men. Am I to conclude that virtually all of the letters written to you on this problem were from men, and if so, what does this say about the difference between men and women?

I did a content analysis of 615 letters sent in response to the second column. I excluded those relatively few cases where the sex of the writer was not apparent and those cases where a group of two or more people was writing. My estimate was that 87% (535/615) of the letter writers were men. I feel safe in inferring that the great preponderance of the letter-writing critics were, in fact, men.

Virginia D. of Sacramento, California recognized this issue in the following letter:

Dear Marilyn,

I find it curious that all the remarks printed in PARADE are from men, especially those who have a title attached to their name. As a member of our male-dominated society, I contend that their name calling and put-downs make a statement as to where these guys are coming from. They are obviously threatened by your status and feel a need to perpetuate the stereotype that women can't be as capable as men. If you were a male touted as having the world's highest IQ, would you have been subjected to the same type of comments? Also, I wonder how many mea culpas you will see. Keep up the great work!

Along the same line, Pat Butler of the National Organization for Women wrote:

Dear Marilyn vos Savant,

Right on! We're circulating your Parade discussion of game-show probabilities and reader response at the NOW headquarters as a clear illustration of the way men deny credibility to women. We also find that people are shaken when "reality clashes with intuition" if intuition supports myths which serve their interests better than fact. Thank you for the pleasure from expanded understanding of probability and the professional feminist amusement your column provided.

Regards and very best wishes.

K.D. of Tempe, Arizona, worried needlessly:

On behalf of women everywhere who really are good at math, I'd like to respectfully request that you not attempt to answer any more mathematical questions. Please stick to more abstract, philosophical problems where there's no absolute right-or-wrong solution. . . .

Even after people explain it, you're still not comprehending the situation. You are single-handedly doing a great deal to perpetuate the "women are no good at math" stereotype. I think you drew yourself off course by getting hung up on numbering the doors. What seems to you to be 3 possibilities is really only 2. . . . Please— no more stupid answers! You're hurting all of us.

Writing to someone else with a copy sent to Marilyn, A.O.A., the author of a book on probability and statistics, commented, "Of course, Marilyn must have consulted someone who really understood the problem before she gave it in her column—after all she's no dummy."

This next letter came from Andrew Bremner of the Department of Pure Mathematics and Statistics of the University of Cambridge with a touch of *noblesse oblige* near the end:

> Dear Marilyn,
> ...your answer that you should switch to door #2 since that has a 2/3 chance of winning, is incorrect. Each of doors #1 and #2 has 1/2 chance of winning. Your analysis of enumerating all possibilities is fool-proof, but you include the cases for
> > GOAT   GOAT   AUTO
> which is known not to occur. The only possibilities are
> > AUTO   GOAT   GOAT
> > > (Switch, lose; stay, win)
> > GOAT   AUTO   GOAT
> > > (Switch, win; stay, lose)
> Your correspondents were rather rude; I wager your womanhood is a factor!
> Yours sincerely,

Much more hostile in tone is this letter from R.L. in Coral Springs, Florida:

Dear Marilyn:

Nowhere in the original question did you state that the host "always" opens a goat door after your initial selection and then asks if you would like to switch. You slipped that condition neatly into your second column. Then, faced with a second avalanche of irate letters, you've decided to call your assumption a condition.

You may have an I.Q. of 610, but you are still a woman, and when faced with a correct answer, a woman will always change the question.

P.S. That picture of that pretty woman attached to your column probably isn't you. **I bet you are a dog!**

The Gamblers

Several letter writers saw how the Monty Hall problem could be converted into a gambling situation. But what should be the stakes and what should be the odds? Here the letter writers differed significantly. A.C. of Pasco, Washington wrote:

> Another letter concerning the doors, goats and cars. I not only believe you are wrong. I know you are wrong. . . . If you can get a disinterested person to run through this exercise 500 times or more, I will bet my next Social Security check that I am right and you are wrong.

H.C. of Tamal, California wrote:

> $20,000 says you're wrong about the game show. . . . After the host shows a goat in 3, you know it was (Auto, goat, goat) or (goat, Auto, goat). You have **new** knowledge at this step that (goat, goat, Auto) is out. As a pro-gambler I see this stuff a lot.

These first two letter writers specified the proposed stakes but not the odds. The next two letter writers agreed upon some rather peculiar odds which they attempted to justify. In effect, they were proposing that if they are right in their understanding of the problem, they win big, but if Marilyn's solution is correct, they break even. People testing a new strategy in Las Vegas might long for such a deal. After committing a very common error among letter writers (see Table 1.1), J.M. of Ithaca, New York, wrote:

> Meditate on the difference between knowledge/wisdom and a very high I.Q. "Savant" denotes learning, not cocksure ignorance. If you still believe you are correct, put your money where your mouth is. Let's play the game. You will, of course, switch each time believing that you will win 2/3 of the time. But we'll use your odds: each time you win I'll give you $10.00; each time you lose you will give me $20.00. If you are right, you will lose nothing in the long run. If I am right I shall receive some meager compensation for taking the time and effort to educate a barely sufferable know-it-all.
> Very truly yours,

W.N. of Livermore, California, wrote similarly, at least regarding the proposed odds:

> It must be ratings season in the Sunday supplement industry. Apparently you're trying to stimulate responses from readers—I can't think of any other plausible reason for your steadfast defense of such a clinker as that claim about the 3-door problem. "My original answer is correct," indeed!
> There are many ways to show that after door 3 reveals a goat, the chance that the prize is behind door 1 now jumps to 1/2. I won't go into the details, that's child's play.
> But let me propose a demonstration which should prove convincing. If you persist in your claim, then you must agree that a fair bet would be for you to offer 2-to-1 odds that your strategy would break even in a long series of tests. I'll be very happy (nay, ecstatic) to mortgage my house and take the other side of that bet. Just let me know when and where you'd like this test to be held.

And you don't need to give me much advance notice of the test, because I won't have to mortgage anything. After the first 15 minutes, we'll be playing on your money.
Keep smiling,
W.N., non-Ph.D.

Directing his comments to the Ph.D.'s who had written critical letters to Marilyn, J.K. an engineer in Bend, Oregon, wrote:

You Ph.D.'s should be ashamed of yourselves as you obviously responded with your mouths instead of your brains. Did you do an in-depth analysis before you responded? I thought that was a basic method taught to your students. Or has something changed since I went to school. . . .

Incidentally, if any of you still doubt Marilyn's answer I will challenge you to play this game with the rules outlined in her February 17, 1991, Parade Magazine column. You will not be allowed to change from your first choice. We will play this game 200 times and for each time you pick the winning door I will give you 100 dollars. Each time you lose because you can't switch to the other door and it is the winning door you will give me 100 dollars. Remember, after you make your choice, one of the other doors will be opened and it will always be a losing door.

Still think her answer and analysis are incorrect? Better think it over real carefully.

The last of our "gambling" writers had yet a somewhat different take on what the odds should be:

I thought the argument you presented originally (regarding the game show problem) was both valid and easily understood. The only real mystery was why are all those math Ph.D.'s having so much trouble with such a simple problem. . . .

But perhaps the apparent simplicity of this problem is just an illusion and they are applying some obscure principle unfamiliar to mere laymen. If I have wronged them, I am prepared to make amends by offering one of them a chance to augment his meager academic salary by playing the following variation of the game you proposed in your column.

The stake for each round of this game will be $100 of which the Ph.D. will put up $45 and I will contribute $55. A host will hide a penny under one of the three cups at random. Of course, only the host knows the location of the penny. The Ph.D. will select one of the cups. The host will then reveal one of the other two cups which does not hide the penny. I will make the remaining cup my choice.

Since the host deliberately chose a losing cup, either the Ph.D. or I have chosen the winning cup and can claim the $100. I am prepared to bring a stake of $10,000 to such a game.

Sincerely, D.L.,
Austin, Texas

D.L. didn't specify the number of rounds to be played, so about the only way the Ph.D. could win would be to get lucky in the early rounds and then quit. If they played 100 rounds, D.L. could expect to win on about 67 of those rounds and gain an expected profit of $1,200 [(67 x 45) minus (33 x 55)].

"Acquaintance" Letters

Shortly after I began reading the letters, I wondered to myself whether I would encounter a letter from someone I know personally and whether that would present any special ethical issue. No, I thought—forgetting temporarily the research on the "small world" phenomenon—it is most unlikely.[2]

---

2 S. Milgram, "The Small World Problem," pp. 259-275 in J. Sabini and M. Silver (Eds.) **The Individual In a Social World**, 1992, New York: McGraw-Hill.

As it turned out, I came across three letters sent in by people I know. The first was from a colleague of mine at the University of Missouri, a chemist who I knew casually through a community theater group. He wrote as follows (in response to the second of Marilyn's columns):

Dear Marilyn:

Sorry, but you blew it again. Using your six possible games: once you have opened the third door to reveal a goat, your original possibilities are reduced to four, because the discovery that there is a goat behind door No. 3 eliminates your original third and sixth combinations. The probabilities have changed because the guesser now has more information than before; what is now facing him or her is:

DOOR 1	DOOR 2
AUTO	GOAT
GOAT	AUTO
AUTO	GOAT
GOAT	AUTO

Now do you see why the guesser's odds have become 1/2?? (*sic*) I should add that I am only needling you because I take special pleasure in finding feet of clay on people I especially admire, such as yourself.
Sincerely,
E.M., Ph.D.

I then wrote a memo to E.M., explaining the problem as best I could, and I enclosed the letters by Steve Selvin plus some other related materials. E.M. responded graciously, thanking me for reawakening his interest in this problem, and assuring me that he didn't mind my "needling." He went on to say that, "we professorial types need to have our egos punctured (preferably gently, as in this case) every once in a while."

The second "acquaintance letter" came from a former student of mine from St. Louis. C.Z. was a very bright young man, a national merit scholar, whose college grades were mediocre due to his activity in a fraternity (my interpretation). C.Z.'s letter referred to Marilyn's reasoning as flawed. He then went on to demonstrate the eight possibilities, requiring the contestant to choose correctly on the first choice 50% of the time (see Table 1.1). He concluded:

> No benefit from switching will be realized. The probability of winning is 1/2 in either case. Your concern with the inability of the odds to go up is explained as follows. If the game ended after your first choice, with no elimination of shells, your chances of winning would be 1/3. With the added variable of the host always eliminating a shell, however, and giving you another chance, your odds of winning are always 1/2 (*sic*).
>
> To err is human (I should know),
>
> C.Z.

My effort to re-contact him proved to be unsuccessful. Chalk it up to the mobility of youth.

The last of my "acquaintance letters" was from Robyn Dawes, a distinguished professor of psychology at Carnegie Mellon University. We met briefly at a conference in Washington D.C., and I was familiar with his research on social judgment. He wrote:

> Dear Ms. vos Savant,
>
> You are, of course, correct on the shell game. . . . One way I have found of persuading people who claim that the probability that the auto is behind the second door can't go up either is to point out that: (i) Opening either the second or third door has no effect on the probability that the auto is behind the first, because if the auto is behind the first door either of the other doors can be opened, but (ii) It does change the probability that the auto is

behind the second door, because only the third door <u>could</u> have been opened if the auto was behind the second. It's basically a "Bayesian" argument.

The "prior" it's behind the first door is 1/3, as is the prior it's behind the second door. Now evidence. The first door cannot be opened. <u>If</u> the auto is behind it, the probability the third door (as opposed to the second) is opened is .50. If the auto is behind the second, the probability the third door is opened is 1.00. Hence, the likelihood ratio of the evidence favoring the second is 2/1. Given the auto cannot now be behind the third door, the equal prior probabilities ("odds") of the auto's being behind the second or the first door modified by this likelihood yield posterior probabilities of 2/3 and 1/3 respectively. In more intuitive terms, the fact the second door <u>wasn't</u> opened changes the probability the auto is behind it, but not the probability the auto is behind the first.

Sincerely,
Robyn M. Dawes
Professor of Psychology

Humorous and Poetic Letters

In addition to the serious letters, which comprised the overwhelming majority, there were several that were written in a more light-hearted vein. In the first, note the date, a few weeks after the Allied Forces had begun their military campaign to oust Iraqi forces from Kuwait, and a few days after Marilyn's third column on the Monty Hall Dilemma.

February 19, 1991

Dear Marilyn,

I have been following the debate about the game show problem with great joy. It is heartening to know that the professors and citizens of your great country can't see the error of their ways. If this is an example of American genius, then I will be victorious. HAHAHAHAHAHA!!!!!!

Sincerely,
Saddam Hussein
Random Bunkers
Somewhere in Iraq

It is, of course, highly improbable that this letter was written by Saddam Hussein, especially in light of the facts that it was post-marked from Boston, and the return address on the envelope indicated it was sent by Robert Scheinerman, Suzanne Reyes, and Susanto Basu of the Department of Economics at Harvard University.

Bob Van Duzer of Santa Barbara, California wrote, "Please consider the following as a helpful explanation."

> Marilyn and you Ph.D.'s
> Upon two things we can agree.
> The host has odds at two to one
> With three closed doors, when the game's begun.
> Also, there's unanimous vote
> That one host door contains a goat.
> Now here's where it gets recondite.
> It's two to one while he's out of sight.
> But don't contend what's downright silly:
> That odds will change when we see ol' Billy.
> Marilyn's right, it's just uncanny
> Switch your choice and avoid that nanny.

Another poem, penned by Bill Hall of Knoxville, Tennessee, capitalized on the many hapless people who got the problem all wrong and also indicated they were the proud owners of the Doctor of Philosophy Degree, the coveted Ph.D.

Marilyn, Marilyn you have been taken to task,
By a group of scholars you forgot to ask,
To solve a problem requiring only logic,
Not great secrets deemed pedagogic.
Your answer's correct, it's easy to see,
For this I needed no advanced degree.
As for the others? If I may surmise please,
Perhaps they couldn't see the forest for their PHD's.

Rudy Fischer of Salem, Oregon chose to focus on the implied value of the car versus the goat:

> I always enjoy your column in Parade and usually agree with your answers. But today's car/hidden goat problem has led you and Ph.D.'s from coast to coast completely astray. The only winner is the person who gets the goat; the car goes to the loser.
>
> Just consider the first year after you win the low average of:
>
> A. A car costs: income tax $2,500, insurance $500, gas, etc. $1,000; Net loss: $4,000.
>
> B. A goat costs: income tax $50; positive cash flow: savings on milk, cheese $98, savings on gas, etc. $12, proceeds on sale of manure, hedge trimmer, lawn mower, etc. $400; Net gain: $460.
>
> Even if this yearly differential of $4,460 declines to half of this for the remaining nine useful years' life for both car and goat, the goat has a relative positive value of $24,530—a clear winner.
>
> For those who may claim that the above is true only if the goat is a female, I point out that it must be, because if the goats behind the doors were males, the contestants would know it all along, even without opening the doors!
>
> Yours truly,
> Rudy Fischer, Ph.D., Illinois, 1951

Along the same line, Nelson Hitchcock of Elberton, Georgia, wrote,

Dear Marilyn:

Your logic is flawless and easily demonstrated. My concern lies in a different direction. As chief spokesman for the GAL (Goat Anti-Defamation League), I must take serious exception to your choice of goats as undesirable prizes. You will be hearing from our attorneys.

Kindest regards,

Nelson Hitchcock, P.t.D. (Part-time Dilettante)

This final letter calls to mind the aphorism from the play, "Inherit the Wind," where the character playing William Jennings Bryant declares, "I am more interested in the Rock of Ages than I am in the age of rocks."[3]

Dear Marilyn,

I am no Ph.D., M.D. or any other D. I am just a Senior Citizen who went to Grade School when it was called Grammar School.

As you can see by the enclosed clipping of a recent column of yours, I have highlighted two instances where you have placed the adverb before the verb. . . . I wish you would write a full column relating to the use of adverbs, since grammar is MUTILATED by so-called professionals every day.

Very Sincerely Yours,

Joe Casale, Las Vegas Nevada

---

3 J. Lawrence and R. Lee, **Inherit the Wind**, 1986, New York: Dramatists Play Service, pp. 56.

CHAPTER 4
SOME INITIAL MONTY HALL STUDIES

I'd rather fight than switch.
Advertising slogan for Tareyton cigarettes

Based on the letters to Marilyn vos Savant, as well as anecdotal observations, we anticipated that people would show a strong tendency to stick with their initial answer when confronted with a two-stage decision. Nevertheless, we thought it wise to reserve judgment until after we had gathered some systematic data. Therefore, we did two initial baseline studies. In these studies we did not manipulate any independent variables. Rather, the purpose was to explore what people actually do when they make a two-stage decision under controlled conditions.

A "Simple" Word Problem

We regarded it as an open question as to how people, other than those who took it upon themselves to write letters, would respond. Therefore, we inserted the Monty Hall Dilemma into a questionnaire administered to two sections of an introductory sociology class at the University of Missouri (N=228). The wording used was drawn almost verbatim from the **New York Times** article by John Tierney.[1] The wording is designed to minimize ambiguity often associated with analyses of the Monty Hall Dilemma. The wording also does a good job of incorporating the crucial assumptions that were specified in Chapter 1. Thus, for instance, Monty Hall states honestly, and in advance that he **will** open one of the losing doors, not that he might or could do so. The wording was as follows:

> Monty Hall, a thoroughly honest game-show host, has placed a new car behind one of three doors. There is a goat behind each of the other doors. "First you point toward a door," he says. "Then I'll open one of the other doors to reveal a goat. After I've shown you the goat, you make your final choice, and you win whatever is behind that door." You begin by pointing to door number 1. Monty then shows you that door 3 has a goat. What would your final choice be?
>
> _____Stick with door 1 _____ Switch to door 2

In this initial study, only 13% (30/226) indicated they would switch to door 2, while 87% (196/226) indicated they would choose to stick with door 1. This indicates a strong propensity to stick when, on rational grounds, the correct answer is to switch. These results are consistent with the hypothesis that the advantage one gains by switching in the Monty Hall Dilemma is counterintuitive. Additional findings rule out some erstwhile explanations.

First, we looked for a possible gender effect, but did not find it. Among men respondents, 15% said switch, compared to 12% of the women respondents. This difference of three percentage points is small enough so it can be reasonably attributed to chance fluctuation. That is, the difference between men and women respondents was not statistically significant in this comparison.

---

1   J. Tierney, "Behind Monty Hall's doors: Puzzle, debate and answers," 1991, July 21, **New York Times**, pp. 1, 20.

Second, we considered whether the tendency to stick in the Monty Hall Dilemma is a reflection of a more general tendency to stay with the **status quo.** Another item on the questionnaire posed a question regarding the respondent's preference regarding the status quo on a matter of considerable importance to the respondents:

> Currently, as you know, final course grades at this university are submitted as A, B, C, D, or F. It has been proposed that we change so that pluses and minuses are recorded and included when calculating the grade point average with an A- figured in at 3.67, B+ at 3.33, B at 3.00, B- at 2.67 and so forth. Would you favor or oppose such a change?
>
> _____favor _____oppose

Opinion on the grading system, an issue that was being currently debated, was split almost right down the middle with 116 (51%) students favoring the change and 112 (49%) opposing the change. However, decisions on the Monty Hall Dilemma were not significantly related to the preference for the status quo in the matter of grades. Of those favoring the change in the grading system, 14% answered switch to door 2, while 13% of those opposing the grading change answered switch on the Monty Hall Dilemma item.

Third, we considered whether answering stick or switch on the Monty Hall Dilemma was related to a more general ability to correctly solve other probability teasers. Therefore, we included in the survey a famous conjunction question, often referred to as the "Linda Problem." The wording we used for the Linda Problem was drawn from an essay by Daniel Kahneman and Amos Tversky[2]:

> Linda is 31 years old, single, outspoken, and very bright. She majored in Philosophy. As a student, she was deeply concerned

---

2   D. Kahneman and A. Tversky, "On the study of statistical intuition," pp. 493-508 in D. Kahneman, P. Slovic, and A. Tversky, **Judgment under Uncertainty: Heuristics and Biases,** 1982, New York: Cambridge University Press.

with issues of discrimination and social justice, and also participated in anti-nuclear demonstrations. Check the alternative which you think is more probable.

_____Linda is a bank teller

_____Linda is a bank teller who is active in the feminist movement

Among our Missouri undergraduates, 86% (196/227) got the Linda problem wrong, checking as more probable, "Linda is a bank teller who is active in the feminist movement." Coincidentally, this was the same percentage as that reported by Kahneman and Tversky in their study of Stanford undergraduates. In our study, of the 31 people who got the Linda problem correct (by checking "Linda is a bank teller"), only 4 (13%) chose to switch on the Monty Hall Dilemma. Among those who got the Linda problem incorrect, 13% (26/195) indicated they would switch on the Monty Hall Dilemma. So these two probability problems appear to be unrelated to one another.

The fourth possibility we considered had to do with a possible link between a student's grade point average (GPA) and how they responded to the Monty Hall Dilemma. GPA is used here as a rough indicator of how bright students are or how seriously they take matters of scholarship. Students were asked to state their grade point average, and most of them did so. However, there was no apparent relationship between GPA and answers to the Monty Hall Dilemma. Overall, students reported an average GPA of 2.87. The same average GPA (2.9) was reported by the 181 students who chose stick on the Monty Hall Dilemma as by the 28 students who chose switch on the Monty Hall Dilemma.

To summarize thus far, this initial vignette provided support for the hypothesis that people tend to stick with their initial answer in the Monty Hall Dilemma even though it would have been in their interest to switch doors for the final answer. The observed split (13-87%) departs radically from what might be expected if the students had answered the Monty Hall question on a haphazard or random basis (50-50). However, several variables were observed to be unsuccessful in differentiating the switchers from those who were inclined to stick. Those variables were gender, preference for a type of grading system, another counterintuitive probability problem, and the respondent's grade point average. In this vignette research, people indicate how they **think** they would respond in a particular hypothetical situation. Next we devised a laboratory study in order to observe people's behavior in the Monty Hall Dilemma when given an incentive to get it right. The laboratory situation provided for observations over numerous trials. Thus, we could test whether people, who are initially inclined to stick when they should switch, can learn the correct solution inductively through repeated plays of this game.

Laboratory Simulation

In our first laboratory study of behavior in the Monty Hall Dilemma, people participated in a computer-administered study. Participants made decisions in a series of 50 trials. This design allows us to observe both the initial propensity to stick or switch (trial 1), and the degree to which inductive learning occurs across trials. In this study, we looked for the possible effects of two variables that are not amenable to manipulation, gender and psychological rigidity. Although gender did not exert a significant effect in the previous study, its effect still might manifest itself in the 50 trial laboratory study.

The other independent variable in this study was psychological rigidity. After examining a large number of personality scales, psychological rigidity seemed to fit most closely the sort of thinking that might cause people to stick with a revocable decision even when it would be rational to switch. Consider, for example, the following items from a standard rigidity scale:

1. I am often the last one to give up trying to do a thing.
2. I dislike to change my plans in the midst of an undertaking.
3. I find it easier to stick to a certain schedule, once I have started on it.

4. I do not enjoy having to adapt myself to new and unusual situations.

5. I always finish tasks I start, even if they are not very important.[3]

The prediction was that psychological rigidity would be inversely correlated with switching on the initial and subsequent trials of the Monty Hall Dilemma.

In this study, 126 undergraduate students (68 women and 58 men) at the University of Missouri served as subjects. The study was conducted in a computer lab. Subjects were not permitted to sit next to one another or to communicate with each other during the session. The experimenter called up a program named "LUMAD" (Let Us Make A Deal). The experimenter states that the study was largely self-administering. Subjects were told they could ask questions of the experimenter at any point if the instructions on the screen were unclear or inadequate.

Subjects were given these instructions:

In this study, you will be asked to make a number of decisions. On each trial you will be shown 3 doors (1, 2, and 3). Behind one of the doors is an ACE that is always considered the "correct" answer, i.e., the winning answer. Behind each of the other doors is a JOKER that is always considered the "incorrect" answer, i.e., the losing answer. On each trial you will begin by guessing which door has the ACE behind it. After you have made your initial guess for a given trial, you will be told that one of the other answers is NOT the correct one. You will then make your final choice for that trial by indicating that you want to STICK with your initial guess or SWITCH to the other remaining door. This same two-step decision procedure will be used over a series of 50 trials. There is no limit to the number of trials on which you can decide to stick or switch.

---

3 These are items from the Gough-Sanford Rigidity Scale. See M. Rokeach, **The Open and Closed Mind**, 1960, New York: Basic Books, pp. 418-419.

The instructions then went on to say:

> After each final decision, you will be shown whether your answer for that trial was correct or incorrect. If you STICK with your original answer and it is the ACE, you will get 1 point. If you SWITCH to the other remaining door and it is the ACE, you will get 1 point. If your answer turns out to be a JOKER, you will get 0 points for that trial, regardless of whether you decided to STICK or SWITCH.

The instructions concluded:

> Your goal should simply be to accumulate as many points as possible during the 50 trials. The situation will be repeated with several people. Of all the people who participate in a given condition, the person who gets the highest point total will get a reward of 25 dollars.

After the 50 trials of the Monty Hall Dilemma, subjects were asked five post-experiment questions concerning the task, (1) whether it was a matter of luck or one that could be analyzed and controlled, (2) whether they had followed a consistent strategy, (3) how lucky or unlucky they had been, (4) whether the situation was fair or rigged, and (5) whether they disliked or enjoyed the task. Each of these questions used a 1-9 rating scale. Using the same type of scale, subjects were also asked 22 questions comprising the Gough-Sanford Rigidity Scale. In answering these 22 items, subjects were asked to think about their life experiences in general rather than focusing on what may have just happened recently.

On trial 1, recording the subject's initial reaction to the Monty Hall Dilemma, only 13 of 126 (10%) subjects decided to switch, which is quite similar to the responses to the word problem result described above. By the time the 50th trial occurred, the percentage who switched had increased to 54% (68/126), indicating a very substantial change. Figure 4.1 shows the percentage switching across the entire series of 50 trials. There it is evident that a significant, nonlinear relationship is observed. Switching began at a very low level, then increased rather sharply, but then seemed to reach a plateau. Once that plateau is reached, very little, if any, further increase in switching is observed. The peak in switching occurred on trial 43 (66%).[4]

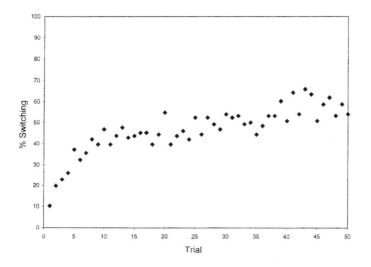

Figure 4.1. Percentage of switching on 50 trials of the Monty Hall Dilemma (N = 126)

If people understand the problem and act rationally, they ought to switch on every trial. If people finish the series of 50 trials by switching on each of the last several trials, we can say that they mastered the problem. We set the standard, therefore, that anyone who switched on each of the last 10 trials was said to have mastered the problem. That difficult standard was met by only 10% (13/126) of the sample.

There was also some connection between what people did on the first trial and what they did on all of the subsequent trials. Those who switched on trial 1 switched an average of 29.1 times on trials 2-50, compared to

4 Similar results were reported by D. Friedman, "Monty Hall's three doors: construction and deconstruction of a choice anomaly," **American Economic Review**, 1998, **88**, No. 4, 933-946.

22.7 times for those who decided to stick on trial 1. This difference is statistically significant, implying that the initial propensity is to some degree a harbinger of things to come.

As to the independent variables we proposed to analyze, it appears that they had little, if any, effect. The initial trial yielded very similar results for women (7/68 or 10% switching) and men (6/58, also 10% switching) subjects. On the last trial, 55% of the men and 53% of the women switched, a difference that is not significant. Over all 50 trials, men switched an average of 24.5 trials, compared to 22.3 for women respondents. However, the difference is not significant. Furthermore, men were about as likely to have mastered the dilemma (10%, 6/58) as were women subjects (10%, 7/68).

Scores on the rigidity scale were divided as nearly as possible into a 30-40-30 split (low, medium, high). The percentage switching on trial 1 was 5% for the low group, 14% for the medium group, and 11% for the high group. On the last trial, the percentage switching was 49% for the low group, 57% for the medium group, and 55% for the high group. Across all 50 trials, the correlation between psychological rigidity and the number of switches was +.11. Overall, the low rigidity subjects switched on an average of 21.9 trials when the possible range was 0-50; those medium on the rigidity scale switched an average of 23.1 trials; and high rigidity subjects switched on an average of 25.0 trials. None of these findings was statistically significant and, in fact, tended to be in the direction opposite from the predicted.

On the first of the five post-experiment questions using a scale from 1-9, subjects made an average rating of 5.0, precisely at the hypothetical midpoint of the scale. This indicates that subjects believed that success in the dilemma is based partly on luck but also partly on control and analysis. On the remaining 4 items, subjects leaned in the direction of claiming that they had played a consistent strategy (5.7), that they had been unlucky (4.6), seeing the situation as fair rather than rigged (4.7), and liking the experience (5.9). Comparing the ratings by men and women, there was only one significant difference. Men were more likely, on average, to claim that they had played a consistent strategy (6.1) than were women (5.4). Similarly, when we compared the 13 people who mastered the problem with the other 113 subjects, only one significant difference appeared on the post-experimental questions. Subjects who had mastered the problem were significantly more likely to see the situation as one that could be analyzed and controlled (6.2) than were the remaining subjects (4.9).

Concluding Comments

Given the results of these two baseline studies, a picture of how people react to being in the Monty Hall Dilemma begins to emerge. In both studies, participants showed a strong tendency to stick when, in fact, this is a non-optimal decision. That finding is put to the test under a wide variety of circumstances in subsequent chapters.

The laboratory study showed what people would do when they had a monetary incentive to get it right. Conceivably, the incentive was not sufficient to get subjects to concentrate their thinking about the problem at hand. That was not our impression, however, in administering the study. Some subjects got out paper and pencil in an attempt to discern a winning pattern. Others lingered after the session was completed to discuss the best strategy. Our impression was that the promise of a $25 prize, later fulfilled, was an attractive yet credible incentive.

It is likely that at least some of the subjects in the laboratory study had a misplaced focus. Told in advance there would be 50 trials, many subjects seemed to be looking for nonrandom sequences in the correct answer across trials rather than focusing on the basic structure of the situation in a given trial. It probably never occurred to most subjects that the optimal solution might be to never switch or to always switch. Most subjects began the 50 trial series by using a mixed strategy. That makes it more difficult to discern the best strategy.

It is also possible that a few subjects may have had the correct sense of the odds but failed to make the correct inference on the optimal behavioral decision. Some who had the odds correct at 2:1 in favor of switching may have concluded that they should lean toward switching 2/3 of the time rather than always switching. This strategy is called **probability matching**. However, by switching on 2/3 of the trials and sticking on 1/3, one wins on about 56% of the trials (2/3 x 2/3) + (1/3 x 1/3). On the other hand, if one always switches, one can expect to win on about 67% (2/3) of the trials.

When subjects play a mixed strategy, it may be difficult to tell the difference between the 2/3 chance of winning by switching and the 1/2 chance of winning by mixing switching and sticking in a 50-50 pattern. People see that when they switch sometimes they win but sometimes they also lose. In the laboratory study, the actual correlation between the number of times the subject switched and the number of points the subject accumulated across 50 trials was +.71. That correlation is not fixed, but rather it depends upon the amount of variation in the number of switches across trials by different people. Nonetheless, if we square that correlation coefficient, it comes out very close to 50%. This means that the success of subjects in this study is determined about 50% by the number of trials they switched on, and the other 50% is due to luck. Such is the beauty of the Monty Hall Dilemma! It accurately reflects real life in one important respect. Success is determined, in good measure by what we do and the decisions we make, but also in good measure by chance events.

One important finding, that we did not anticipate, occurred when the subjects reached a plateau. Subjects began the series at a very low level of switching, about 10%, increased rapidly their level of switching to about 55%, but then they reached a plateau and did not show any further improvement.

This calls to mind the concept of **satisficing**, a concept coined by Herbert Simon, a Nobel Prize winner in economics.[5] It refers to a situation in which people experience a satisfactory level of success and are satisfied with that rather than striving for an ideal or optimal solution.

In another context, Roger Tourangeau suggested that the likelihood of satisficing (LS) is equal to task difficulty (TD) divided by the product

---

5 H. Simon, "Rational choice and the structure of the environment," **Psychological Review**, 1956, **63**, No. 2, 129-138.

of ability (A) and motivation (M): LS=TD/(A x M).[6] Hence, satisficing would be directly correlated with the difficulty of the task, but inversely with ability and motivation. One would expect less satisficing if the problem were more tractable, if the incentive to do well were increased, and if the aptitude of the subjects were somewhat higher. All this sounds plausible, but its speculative character should be apparent. Our laboratory simulation of the Monty Hall Dilemma may provide for studying rational and irrational tendencies in two-stage decision making.

Perhaps it can also bear relevance to the psychological processes thought to attend decision making. Leon Festinger's theory of cognitive dissonance held that the interesting psychological processes of subjective distortion, selectivity, and dissonance reduction occur only after a final and irrevocable decision has been made.[7] It may be that this view is partially incorrect in that there may be some intriguing processes that occur after a preliminary and entirely revocable decision has been made. Even when people have no good reason for their initial selection, having acted upon it, they may become psychologically bound or committed to it.[8]

A valid concern is whether the results obtained in the laboratory study have any implications for decisions in everyday life. My view is that the two-stage decision, in which one makes a tentative decision, gains additional information, and then makes a final commitment, is very common if indeed not the rule. On Friday night, an investor tentatively decides to buy shares in a particular company, but searches for relevant information prior to actually investing the money the following Monday. If we knew that people have an irrational tendency to stick with an initial decision when they ought to switch, this would obviously be an important principle.

---

6 Cited in J. Krosnick, "Response strategies for coping with the cognitive demands of attitude measures in surveys," **Applied Cognitive Psychology**, 1991, **5**, 213-236.

7 L. Festinger, **Conflict, Decision and Dissonance**, 1964, Stanford, CA: Stanford University Press.

8 J. Russo, V. Medvec, and M. Meloy, "The distortion of information during decisions," **Organizational Behavior and Human Decision Process**, 1996, **66**, No. 1, 102-110; C. Kiesler, **The Psychology of Commitment**, 1971, New York: Academic Press.

On the other hand, the Monty Hall Dilemma may be difficult for people to solve precisely because it is so uniquely contrived. Aside from the game-show context, it is not easy to come up with a situation in which people receive **valid information about unchosen alternatives from a knowledgeable host** after a tentative decision but prior to a final decision. Richard Henshel has argued that experiments in social psychology should deliberately create situations that would never occur under natural circumstances.[9] Indeed, that may have been done in the Monty Hall Dilemma.

---

9 R. Henshel, "The purpose of laboratory experimentation and the virtues of deliberate artificiality," **Journal of Experimental Social Psychology**, 1980, **16**, No. 5, 466-478.

PART TWO

Empirical Studies of the Monty Hall Dilemma

CHAPTER 5
THE RUSSIAN ROULETTE DILEMMA

From those who wrote letters to Marilyn vos Savant criticizing her 2/3 solution, and the choices made by undergraduate students in our word problem and laboratory studies, it was definitely our impression that in the Monty Hall Dilemma, people show a strong initial tendency to stick with a decision when they should switch. What we lacked at that point was an empirical benchmark, some other data point with which to compare our results.

In the social sciences, case studies can carry us only so far. Comparison has been described as the essence of social research. Or at least it is an essential feature of that enterprise.

For our purposes, we needed a situation that would be quite comparable to the Monty Hall Dilemma, but in which it is rational for a person to stick with a preliminary decision. We wondered what people would do in a situation like that. We knew by then that people had a strong propensity to stick when they should switch. Would they also stick when they should stick? Or, more perversely, would they switch when they should stick? To address this question empirically, we had to find or devise a situation, preferably one that is symmetrical to the Monty Hall Dilemma, in which it is just as rational to stick as it is to switch in the Monty Hall Dilemma.

The Monty Hall Dilemma features one car and two goats. It is established that following an initial selection and the deliberate, planned showing of an incorrect, unchosen door with a goat, one should abandon the initial selection, switching to the remaining door. However, what if we invert the problem so there are two cars and only one goat behind the three doors? In this version, the contestant would choose among three doors. Two of the doors are winners and only one is a loser. We call this inverted Monty Hall problem the Russian Roulette Dilemma**. In Russian Roulette,** a judge presents a convict with a six-chamber revolver and a freedom or death proposition. Only one chamber contains a bullet and the other five are all winners, i.e., they are empty. The math part is clear, and the wording of the Roulette Dilemma is given below.

The probability that the chamber a convict selected was empty is 5/6. That probability does not change when the judge **knowingly** names four other chambers that are empty. If the convict sticks with his initial choice, he is not guaranteed to be set free, but his chances are very good (5/6). Under the circumstances, he cannot do better than that. Switch to the remaining chamber and the chances of self-execution are 5/6, while he would have only 1 chance in 6 of being set free.

If we change back to game show format and from six chambers back to three doors, the Roulette Dilemma can be stated thus:

> Suppose you are on a game show. The host, who is known to be completely honest, has placed a new car behind two of three doors. There is a goat behind the other door. "First, you point toward a door," the host says. "Then I will randomly open one of the other doors to reveal a car and that door will no longer be available. After I have shown you that car, you make your final choice, and you win whatever is behind that door." You begin by pointing to a door, say door number 1. The host then shows you that one of the other doors, say door number 3, has a car. What would your final choice be? Would you stick with door 1 or switch to door 2?

Here, as with the Monty Hall Dilemma, we must be alert to what key assumptions must be made. Of course, an attempt was made to build these assumptions into the wording of the problem. For this to be a true Roulette Dilemma, we must assume that the host is honest, knowledgeable, and committed to the procedure as stated. Under these circumstances, it is rational to stick with one's initial guess. The probability of one's initial guess being a car is 2/3, and this is in no way altered by a host **knowingly** opening one of the other doors to show a car after you make your initial decision. Thus, in the three-door Roulette Dilemma, the chance of winning by switching is only 1/3, while the chances of winning by sticking with one's initial guess are 2/3.

A close reading of some early literature on this type of problem made it relatively easy to derive the Roulette Dilemma. The Monty Hall Dilemma is structurally very similar, at least in terms of probabilities, to the Three Prisoner Problem presented by Martin Gardner in his "Mathematical Games" column in the October 1959 issue of **Scientific American**.[1]

It seems like a small matter to invert that problem so that two of the prisoners are to be pardoned and only one is to be executed. In fact, Gardner did just that when he discussed the situation further, specifically describing one variation in which the chances of avoiding death were 51/52. Mosteller's version of the three prisoners' problem had two of the three prisoners going free.[2]

What is distinctive about the Monty Hall and Russian Roulette dilemmas, in comparison to the Three Prisoner Problem, is the possibility of switching or sticking in a two-stage decision format. As conventionally stated, the Three Prisoner Problem has the probabilities but not the opportunity to stick or switch.

How Do People Choose in the Monty Hall and Roulette Dilemmas?

Using the Monty Hall and Roulette dilemmas together, we have devised a two-stage decision in which it is rational to switch and a comparable situation in which it is rational to stick with one's initial decision. The

1   M. Gardner, "Mathematical games: Problems involving questions of probability and ambiguity," **Scientific American**, 1959, **201** No. 4, 174-182. M. Gardner, "Mathematical games: How three mathematicians disproved a celebrated conjecture of Leonard Euler," **Scientific American**, 1959, **201**, No. 5, 181-188.

2   F. Mosteller, **Fifty Challenging Problems in Probability with Solutions**. 1965, Reading, MA: Addison-Wesley.

two dilemmas are perfectly symmetrical with respect to one another. In both instances the probability of winning is either 1/3 or 2/3. Furthermore, we know exactly what people should do in these dilemmas, but now the question is what people actually do.

The answer is that they do many things, i.e., there is great variety or "diversity" in their responses. Nonetheless, as we shall see, there are signs of coherence and order, albeit not of a simple variety.

We have used the Roulette Dilemma in three different studies. Two of them were word problems, single-trial studies which will be described in Chapters 6 and 7. The third was a laboratory experiment in which people played either the Monty Hall Dilemma or the Russian Roulette Dilemma over 50 trials. Each of the 84 undergraduate subjects in this experiment was randomly assigned to play one game or the other. They were given clear, complete, and non-deceptive instructions before beginning, and direct feedback immediately after each trial was completed. The computer played the role of host. They were also told that the person in each condition who did the best, i.e., located an ACE correctly the largest number of times, would receive a prize of $25. This, together with the intrinsic interest in the problem, seemed to provide adequate motivation so that people made a real effort to do well.

As in previous studies, very few people chose to switch on their initial encounter with the Monty Hall Dilemma. In this experiment, only 8% (3/39) decided to switch on trial 1 of the Monty Hall Dilemma. However, in the Roulette Dilemma, 31% (14/45) switched on trial one. The difference between these percentages is statistically significant—which means that the difference is larger than can be reasonably attributed to chance fluctuation. This effect has not yet been replicated, and it really should be before we make too much of it. However, let us assume for the moment the effect is reliable and try to explain it.

Why should we obtain results that are in the opposite direction from what would be implied by rational processes? That is, people are not at all likely to switch when it is in their rational self-interest to do so, but they are more likely to switch when it is in their interest to stick!

One possible line of explanation involves a **momentum** hypothesis. Consider how things appear to be developing differently in the two dilemmas. In the Monty Hall Dilemma, I pick one door, and then the host shows me that one of the doors that I did not choose is a loser. I might reason, "Thus far, it seems that my guess is not incorrect. Maybe I had better stick with it." On the other hand, in the Roulette Dilemma, I pick one door, and then the host shows me that one of the doors that I did not choose was a winner. I might reason, "Thus far, it seems that my guess is less likely to be correct than it originally was. Perhaps I had better abandon it."

While the results on trial 1 were significant, they should not be overstated. It was not the case that subjects in the Roulette Dilemma chose to switch while those in the Monty Hall Dilemma chose to stick. People in both conditions tended to stick with their initial choice, but this tendency was significantly stronger in the Monty Hall Dilemma. At the same time, subjects in both conditions departed significantly from a 50-50 chance split in the direction of sticking.

How does this compare with what people did on the very last trial? By this time, they had played 49 trials with feedback that could have been enough to encourage switching in the Monty Hall Dilemma and sticking in the Roulette Dilemma. On trial 50, 51% (20/39) switched in the Monty Hall Dilemma, and 33% (15/45) switched in the Roulette Dilemma. Using the rational standard to compare trial 1 and 50, the percentage switching in the Monty Hall Dilemma increased dramatically from a low of 8% to 51%. On the other hand, the percentage of sticking in the Roulette Dilemma stayed about the same, 69% on trial 1 and 67% on trial 50.

The second mode of analysis also looks for a trend across trials, but uses more of the data. The 50 trials were divided into 5 blocks of 10 trials each. The dependent variable was the number of switching choices, and the data are depicted in Figure 5.1. The responses to these dilemmas are remarkably different. Despite the fact that the two dilemmas are perfectly symmetrical to one another in design, the decisions that they elicit are most asymmetrical.

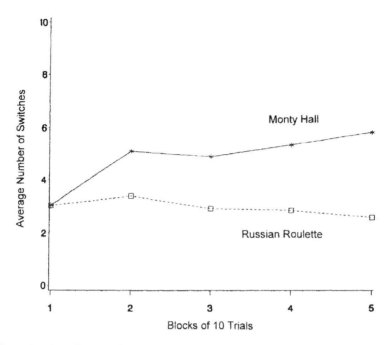

Figure 5.1. Baseline conditions for Monty Hall and Russian Roulette Dilemmas

The percentage switching increased significantly across blocks in the Monty Hall Dilemma, but not at a constant rate. The most significant increase occurred from block 1 to block 2. The differences between blocks 2 and 3, 3 and 4, and 4 and 5 were slight and not significant. The difference between blocks 1 and 5 was significant. The percentage of decisions that were switches increased from 31% on block 1 to 49% on block 2, 49% on block 3, 54% on block 4, and 58% on block 5.

The results for the Roulette Dilemma will be given in terms of percentage sticking since that is the rational standard. Subjects in the Roulette Dilemma began by sticking on 70% of the decisions in block 1, and then continued at about that same level. They recorded 66% sticking on block 2, 71% on block 3, 71% on block 4, and 74% on block 5. None of the differences between adjacent blocks in the Roulette Dilemma was significant. Moreover, the difference between block 1 and block 5 was not significant either.

Putting these results in words, the Roulette subjects were closer to their rational solution of sticking at both the beginning and the end of the series than the Monty Hall subjects were to their correct solution of switching. Stated differently, the Roulette subjects were rather close to a correct solution on the beginning trials but came no closer through the experience of playing the game with feedback for 50 trials. The Monty Hall subjects, on the other hand, were not close to a correct solution on the opening trials but came somewhat closer through experience.

The two conditions shared the feature of displaying a plateau in their choice pattern. For the Roulette subjects, the whole pattern of results is a plateau with no significant improvement across trials. The Monty Hall subjects seemed to reach a plateau after about 20 trials with little improvement thereafter.

It is evident in Figure 5.1 that people do respond differently to the two dilemmas. It is also apparent that this difference increases across the blocks of trials. This can be tapped by looking at the eta coefficients for each block. The eta coefficient can vary from .00 if there is no difference between conditions to 1.00 if the conditions were completely different. The eta values were .00, .28, .36, .46, and .52 for blocks 1-5, respectively. Overall, subjects in the Roulette condition switched an average of 14.8 times on the 50 trials, compared to 24.1 times for the Monty Hall condition.

Reference was made earlier to the diversity of responses to these dilemmas. Table 5.1 shows this by displaying the distribution of subjects across the possible range of responses which could go from 0 to 50 switches. It can be seen that none of the subjects switched on all 50 trials, but there was one subject in the Roulette condition who decided to stick on all 50 trials. The standard deviations for the number of switches were slightly higher for the Monty Hall condition, 9.78, than for the Roulette condition, 9.10. These standard deviations should be considered in relation to the minimum and maximum. The minimum standard deviation is, of course, zero, but that could be obtained only if every subject in a given condition switched the same number of times over 50 trials. The maximum standard deviation, given the possible range of 0-50, is 25. That would be obtained only if half of the subjects decided to stick on every trial and half decided to switch on every trial. This is important to consider because it is probably easier to detect the actual probabilities if one sticks or switches consistently across trials.

Table 5.1.

Distribution of People in the Monty Hall and Roulette Dilemmas

Number of Stays	Monty Hall Dilemma	Roulette Dilemma	Number of Stays	Monty Hall Dilemma	Roulette Dilemma
0	0	0	26	2	2
1	0	0	27	2	2
2	0	0	28	2	2
3	0	0	29	1	1
4	0	0	30	1	1
5	1	0	31	2	2
6	0	0	32	2	0
7	0	0	33	2	2
8	1	0	34	1	0
9	0	0	35	0	2
10	0	0	36	0	1
11	1	0	37	0	0
12	0	0	38	0	4
13	1	0	39	0	2
14	1	0	40	1	3
15	1	0	41	0	1
16	0	0	42	1	2
17	0	0	43	1	0
18	1	0	44	0	3
19	2	0	45	0	2
20	0	3	46	1	1
21	3	0	47	1	3
22	3	1	48	0	1
23	2	1	49	0	0
24	2	0	50	0	1
25	0	1			

Mean = 25.9	Mean = 35.2
N = 39	N = 45
SD = 9.8	SD = 9.1

Most people, as Table 5.1 makes clear, play a mixed strategy of sticking some of the time and switching some of the time. That probably makes it more difficult to discern the pattern and to come up with a winning strategy. Also, it may never have occurred to most subjects that it might be best to always stick or always switch on each trial. This is especially so since switching in the Monty Hall Dilemma or sticking in the Roulette Dilemma, does not guarantee a hit, but rather only makes the odds of winning 2:1.

From the perspective of the participants, it is meaningful to ask just what the actual correlation was between how often a person switched and how many times the person correctly found the ACE. In fact, that correlation was +.65 in the Monty Hall condition and -.57 in the Roulette condition. The magnitude of that correlation depends upon how much variation people show in the number of switches. If the variation were smaller, the correlation would be smaller. If the variation had been larger, the correlation would have been larger. Recall that while there was considerable variation within each condition, the observed variation in the number of switches was still less than half of the maximum possible standard deviation, 39% (9.78/25) in the Monty Hall condition and 36% (9.10/25) in the Roulette condition.

We also considered how many of the subjects mastered the problem. Our difficult standard was whether the person switched on all of the last ten trials in the Monty Hall Dilemma or decided to stick on all of the last ten trials in the Roulette Dilemma. By this standard, only 13% (5/39) mastered the Monty Hall Dilemma, compared to the slightly higher figure of 20% (9/45) for the Roulette Dilemma. The difference between these two percentages is not significant. This tells us that, at least by this standard, subjects were not significantly more likely to finish the series by mastering the Roulette Dilemma than they were the Monty Hall Dilemma. This was so despite an apparent "head start" when subjects began the series closer to the correct standard in the Roulette Dilemma.

Of course, we do not know for sure from this that these 14 subjects who mastered their respective problem actually or fully understood the dilemma in all its nuances. All we know for sure is that they acted, i.e., chose, the way that would be expected of those who did understand fully.

What Does This Experiment Tell Us?

To highlight the results of this experiment, it is apparent that people respond differently to the Monty Hall and the Russian Roulette dilemmas. This is despite the fact that they are structurally the symmetrical counterpart of one another. The differences that were observed were not in a rational mode. People began their encounters by switching more in the Roulette Dilemma, when by rational considerations they should have switched less.

The trend across time indicates that the correct solutions of always switching in the Monty Hall Dilemma and always sticking in the Roulette Dilemma are not easy to learn inductively. Even though it is hazardous to extrapolate far beyond the 50th trial to speculate what would have happened had the series continued, it is not easy to see how a more optimal solution could have been obtained without some further intervention.

Subjects in the Monty Hall Dilemma showed some improvement early in the series, but then reached a plateau and more or less stayed there. Perhaps they were doing about as well as they expected or they may have doubted that they could improve. This view may have caused them to "shut down," so to speak, in the sense that they may have stopped thinking about searching for a better, more optimal solution. The same can be said for the Roulette subjects, except in their case the plateau was there almost from the outset. Future research, in addition to extending the series beyond 50 trials, might also give more informative feedback, increase motivation, recruit subjects with more analytical ability, and, in some way, make the situation more tractable. Also, it would be desirable to have conditions in which subjects play one dilemma for 50 trials and then the other dilemma for 50 trials.

CHAPTER 6
THE HOST'S PROTOCOL

In what we regard as the **Standard** Monty Hall Dilemma, there are no crucial decisions to be made by the host. That is, the host does **not** make a decision on a case by case basis whether to show the contents of an incorrect, unchosen door after the contestant makes a preliminary guess of which door is the winner. The host does **not** make a decision whether to offer the contestant a choice to stick or switch.

In fact, the role of the host could be carried out by an automaton following a basic set of rules. In our laboratory experiments, we do just that. The role of host is played by the computer. The computer as host follows this fixed procedure:

> A. After instructing the subject on the precise procedure to be followed, the computer picks randomly one of the three doors as the winner.
> B. The computer invites the subject to make a preliminary guess, recording that guess.
> C. Taking the results of steps A and B into account, the computer opens and displays the contents of an unchosen, incorrect door. If the subject's initial guess is incorrect, there is only one other incorrect

door, and that is the one that gets opened. For example, if door 2 is the winner, and the subject chooses door 3, door 1 gets opened as that is the only remaining door which is both unchosen and incorrect. When the subject's initial guess is correct, the computer chooses randomly with equal probability which door to open, e.g., if door 2 is the winner, and the subject chose door 2, the computer chooses randomly whether to display the contents of door 1 or door 3.

D. The computer then invites the subject to stick or switch, and then compares the winning door with the subject's final choice. The computer then displays the contents of all three doors and declares whether the subject was correct on that trial.

If one wishes to use the standard form to see how normal people respond naturally to such a dilemma, it is essential that the procedure to be followed be described forthrightly to the subjects, and as completely as possible, **in advance**. If one wishes to deviate from the standard form, that is, to try some variant, there are literally hundreds of possibilities.

For example, one letter writer asked what happens if there is a time limit within which the contestant must choose. The contestant becomes so nervous and excited that he stutters and doesn't make an audible guess within the allotted time. The host goes ahead and opens an incorrect, i.e., non-winning, door which is not the one the contestant intended to choose. Of the remaining two doors, should the contestant stick with his **intended** choice or is it to his advantage to switch to the other remaining door? The answer is that it doesn't matter. His chance of winning is 1/2 regardless of whether he switches or sticks with his intended choice. For the 2/3 solution to obtain, the host must know the contestant's initial guess, and take that into account in determining which incorrect door to open.

Joseph Moder of the University of Miami posed this delightful question in a letter to Marilyn vos Savant:

In the Three Door Game Show, suppose the contestant picks a door as usual, but as the host reaches to open one of the other doors, he suddenly realizes that he has neglected to learn where the prize is. In the spirit of "the show must go on," he unhesitatingly flings open one of the other two doors, and much to his relief, it does not expose the prize. No one, except the host himself, knew of the impetuous act he had just performed; the show went on exactly as it always had. Now . . . can the contestant improve his chances by switching doors?

Strange as it may seem, the answer is no. As indicated previously, the 2/3 solution to the Monty Hall Dilemma depends upon the host knowing where the prize **is and** also knowing the contestant's initial pick. Furthermore, it is essential that the host not only has this knowledge but also that he uses that knowledge in deciding which door to open. It is easy to imagine a set of circumstances in which the host knew but didn't use his knowledge. Marilyn vos Savant's wording made the host's knowledge of the prize location explicit, and left us to presume that the host would know the guest's initial selection, and would use that knowledge in order to assure that a goat would be revealed behind the unchosen door that is opened. An **agnostic** (without knowledge) host could do what appears to be exactly the same thing, e.g., show door 3 with a goat and then offer the choice to stick or switch, but if the selection by the host was based on chance or luck rather than knowledge, the effect is different. This important point is difficult to comprehend fully, but consider these two scenes:

I. A deck of cards is placed face down in a random array on a table. You guess which one is the ace of spades by putting your finger on a card without turning it over. Taking this guess into account, the host, who knows where the ace of spades is, proceeds to turn over 50 cards, none of which is the ace of spades. The host then gives you a choice between sticking with your initial guess or switching to the only other card which is still face down.

II. A deck of cards is placed face down in a random array on a table. You guess which one is the ace of spades by putting your finger on a card without turning it over. The host then invites 50 other people, none of whom knows the location of the ace of spades, to each turn over one card. By chance, none of the cards turned over is the ace of spades. The host then gives you a choice between sticking with your initial guess or switching to the only other card which is still face down.

Even though the initial and final choices appear to be essentially the same, the prevailing probabilities are radically different. Under Scene I, it is rational to switch, provided the other assumptions of the Monty Hall Dilemma are in effect, since the chances of winning by switching are 51/52, compared to a chance of only 1/52 by sticking. On the other hand, under Scene II, it does not matter what one decides, since the odds are even at 50:50 regardless of whether one decides to switch or stick.

J.H., an engineering professor at a university in the state of Washington, wrote to disagree with Marilyn's 2/3 solution to the Monty Hall Dilemma and offered this metaphor:

Imagine three runners in the 100 meter dash. The runners are so evenly matched that the odds of any given runner winning are completely random. I am asked to guess the winner and select runner number 1. After making my choice, runner number 3 pulls a hamstring and cannot compete. Based on your answer to the game show problem, I would conclude that the unfortunate injury to runner number 3 has somehow inexplicably made runner number 2 the clear favorite over my original choice. By way of the above example, I hope it is now clear that your analysis of the game show problem is flawed.

A similar analogy was sent by H.S. of Greer, South Carolina:

. . . picture a horse race with three horses, numbers 1, 2 and 3. Other things being equal, if horse number 3 drops dead 50 feet into the one mile race, the chances of each of the remaining horses winning the race are no longer 1 in 3 but are now 1 in 2. If this scenario is repeated enough times . . . then horse number 1 and horse number 2 will have a near equal number of victories.

These writers are correct in a limited sense, but the implication that their anecdotes comprise a sound analogy to the Monty Hall Dilemma is **fatally flawed.** As an academician might say, the two situations are **not isomorphic**. A key feature of the Monty Hall Dilemma has been omitted, namely, the knowledgeable host. An alternative, more satisfactory, wording of the racing metaphor might be:

> Suppose you have bet on horse number 1 in a 3 horse race in which there is no favorite. After you have placed your bet, omniscient God who, of course, knows the horse destined to win, as well as how you have bet, tells you, "It's not going to be horse number 3." Depending on God's other attributes, e.g., whether God seeks to guide people toward the right decisions, you should probably switch to horse number 2 if you have the opportunity.

The importance of the **knowledgeable** host is not even apparent to some people who agree with vos Savant's 2/3 solution and give otherwise clever and insightful comments. For instance, James Simmons, a mathematician at the University of Virginia, wrote:

> I was amused by the elaborate attempts to explain the best strategy to use in the game-show contest. . . . ("It wasn't until I started writing a computer program. . . .") If I am the contestant and my strategy is always to stick with my initial choice, then the probability that I win is 1/3. If my strategy is always to switch, then the probability that I lose is 1/3, since I lose only if the car is behind the door I first choose. As I either win or lose every time I play, the probability that I win using the switching strategy is 2/3.

Simmons' solution is correct, but only provided we assume the host to be knowledgeable, and that the host uses that knowledge to expose a goat behind one of the unchosen doors after the initial selection.

In her third column on the subject of the Monty Hall Dilemma, Marilyn vos Savant suggested that people do an empirical test over several trials to test first hand her 2/3 solution. In response to her invitation, many people wrote to her reporting on the results of a simulation of one sort or another. Many people reported having done a computer simulation and sent along a printout or a computer disk. An especially valuable one was sent by Joseph Heiser of the Mathematics Department of the Pemberton, New Jersey, High School (see Appendix C). It includes two simulations, building into them the assumption of the knowledgeable host, where the 2/3 solution works, or the agnostic host, where the 1/2 solution works. Juxtaposing the results of these programs demonstrates to many doubters the importance of this distinction.

Of course, people do not always make the assumptions precisely as they are in what we call the Monty Hall Standard condition. At times the dilemma has been stated in an ambiguous manner so that other assumptions are just as plausible. Strictly speaking, the knowledgeable host dutifully opening an unchosen, incorrect door and then giving the contestant the opportunity to switch doors is only one possibility among many. Furthermore, the knowledgeable and agnostic hosts do not, by any means, exhaust the possibilities.

A few letter writers claimed that it is important to know and take into account the motives of the host. That is true only if the host has some discretion, e.g., deciding whether to open an unchosen door and whether to offer the contestant the chance to switch doors. In the standard version of the Monty Hall Dilemma, the motivation of the host is **irrelevant**, since he has no discretion, but rather is following a fixed protocol. Some critics of Marilyn have even suggested that perhaps the host has some special affinity to open a certain door. For instance, the host could be predisposed to open door 3 whenever it is unchosen and incorrect. That contrivance, however, seems a bit far-fetched or at least is stretching things somewhat.

In vos Savant's wording of the problem, we are not told anything about the motivation of the host, and the wording is at least somewhat ambiguous in certain respects. However, it does not follow that the laws of probability apply only when the host selects a door to open at random. The laws of probability also apply to the situation involving a knowledgeable host so long as the host is committed to using that knowledge to open an unchosen, incorrect door and to providing the option to stick or switch. Under these conditions, the probabilities suggested by vos Savant (2/3 for winning by switching and 1/3 for winning by sticking) prevail. The key here is that the host's procedure is fixed in advance and therefore, not a matter of whim or some personality quirk of the host. It is in that sense that the host's motivation is irrelevant in the Monty Hall Standard condition.

If the host has discretion whether to open an unchosen, incorrect door, and whether to offer the choice of switching or sticking, then the situation becomes more complicated. In that case, knowing the motivation of the host would be of value and ought to enter as one of the factors in deciding whether to stick or switch. At the extremes of motivation, consider the cases of the **stingy**, devious host and the **generous**, helpful host.

The stingy host tries to minimize costs and the chances of the contestant winning, and consequently only offers the option of switching when the contestant's initial guess is correct. Of course, if this became known, the smart contestant would never switch, and her probability of winning when the option to switch is offered would be 1.0 by sticking and .00 by switching. The option to switch would become irrelevant, and the overall chance of winning would be 1/3.

The generous host is eager to help the contestant find the car and only provides the option to switch when the contestant's initial guess is incorrect. If this became known, the smart contestant would always switch since the probability of winning when the option is offered would be 1.0 by switching and .00 by sticking. With a generous host whose rules for proceeding, i.e., his protocol, are known, the smart contestant wins every time.

Between these two extremes is a multitude of motivational orientations for the host. For instance, the **indifferent** host flips a coin to decide whether to proceed to the second stage in which an incorrect door is knowingly opened and the guest is given the choice of whether to stick or switch. When an indifferent but knowledgeable host offers the choice to switch or stick, one wins with a probability of 2/3 when switching and 1/3 by sticking.

It is important to emphasize, however, that the host's motives and preferences are **irrelevant** when the host is following the script of the Standard Monty Hall Dilemma in which he has no discretion over the decision about what to do next. Just how sensitive people are to variations in the host's protocol is an open question at this point, one that is subject to empirical investigation.

Two Experiments on the Protocol of the Host

We have done two word problem experiments in which the focus has been on the protocol of the host. Having worked on the problem for some time, one of our hunches was that people seemed to ignore, or at least do not take into account adequately, the knowledge of the host as a cue in trying to come up with a solution. We sought to demonstrate this via a word problem experiment.

If the question is why most people initially get the Monty Hall Dilemma wrong, the first answer is that they misapprehend the true probabilities in the situation. The reason they do this is, first and foremost, because they fail to take into account the importance of the knowledge of the host and how that knowledge is used.

In a survey of 354 college students at the University of Missouri, a Monty Hall type of word problem was used.[1] Respondents received one of four forms distributed in a random manner. A 2 x 2 factorial design was used. The scenario was written to describe one of two gaming situations, the Monty Hall or the Russian Roulette Dilemma as differentiated in the preceding chapter. The wording also included information that described the host as being either knowledgeable (Gnostic)

---

1   D. Granberg and T. Brown, "The Monty Hall Dilemma," **Personality and Social Psychology Bulletin**, 1995, **21**, No. 7, 711-723, Study 4.

or without knowledge (Agnostic) concerning the crucial information, namely, the location of the prize and the contestant's initial selection. In addition to being asked whether they would stick or switch, subjects were asked to give the reasons for their choices and to estimate the probability of winning at two points, after their initial selection and after their final choice. Inasmuch as the wording is very crucial in problems like this, the full wording is given for each of the four conditions in Appendix D.

The rational solution is to switch in the Monty Hall-Gnostic condition and to stick in the Roulette-Gnostic condition. In the two conditions with an Agnostic host, it is a toss-up, i.e., a 50-50 proposition. Table 6.1 shows that the results are not anywhere close to this rational standard.

Table 6.1

Summary of Results from Word Problem Study

	Condition			
	Monty-Gnostic	Monty-Agnostic	Roulette-Gnostic	Roulette-Agnostic
% Switching	15	10	16	4
Average Estimated Probability After Initial Selection	.368	.347	.492	.471
After Final Selection	.528	.492	.482	.505

Note: The four experimental conditions were manipulated by instructions and are described in the text.

In the Monty Hall-Gnostic condition, 15% said switch, compared to 10% in the Monty Hall-Agnostic condition. This difference of 5 percentage points is not significant. In the Roulette-Gnostic condition, 84% said stick, compared to fully 96% who said stick in the Roulette-Agnostic condition. This difference of 12 percentage points is statistically significant.

A strong majority of the people in the Roulette-Gnostic condition was, therefore, deciding correctly, but the difference between the two Roulette conditions was in the opposite direction from rationality. That is, the Roulette-Agnostic subjects were more likely to stick, even though they had less justification for sticking, than the Roulette-Gnostic subjects. Also, in this study, the Monty Hall-Gnostic subjects did not differ significantly from the Roulette-Gnostic subjects in the likelihood of their switching. Overall, the Agnostic host produced less switching than the Gnostic host.

The average estimates of the probability of being correct after stage 1 and after stage 2 decisions are also given in Table 6.1. The effect of the type of game (Monty Hall vs. Roulette) was highly significant in the estimates of the probability of being correct after the initial selection. Even so, it is surprising that the estimated probability for the Monty Hall conditions was close to .33 (ave.=.36), but the average estimate for the Roulette conditions (.48) was not close to .67. The four conditions all hovered near an average of .50 after the stage 2 decision and were not significantly different from one another.

In the Monty Hall-Gnostic condition, by far the most common pattern of answers was to give .33 and then .50 as the two estimates of probability. This specific pattern was shown by 44% of the subjects in this condition. Finally, we checked to see whether people who said switch gave different estimates of the probabilities than people who said stick. It appears that they did. For instance, in the Monty Hall-Gnostic condition, the minority who said switch did not differ significantly from the majority who said stick in their estimates of the probability after the initial selection, but in the estimates of the final probability, the switchers gave significantly higher estimates (ave.=.61) than those who decided to stick (ave.=.51).

Overall, the results of this word problem experiment support the hypothesis that people do not take into account adequately the knowledgeable host cue. This interpretation is reinforced by the open-ended comments made by these subjects. Comments by subjects in the Gnostic conditions are not noticeably different from those of subjects in the Agnostic conditions. This is despite the fact that this manipulation has a radical effect on the nature of the dilemma and fundamentally alters the structure of the situation.

In the second word problem experiment, also conducted with University of Missouri students, subjects received one of three basic problem versions.[2] Each version had a conceptually distinct logical structure but corresponded, in surface manifestation, to the Monty Hall Dilemma. In all three versions, the instructions indicated a prize behind one of three doors with the subject given the option of switching her choice from door 1 to door 2 after the host revealed that door 3 did not contain the prize. Subjects in each case were asked whether it was best to stick or switch. All three versions began with the same introduction:

> A thoroughly honest game-show host has placed a car behind one of three doors. There is a goat behind each of the other doors. You have no prior knowledge that allows you to distinguish among the doors.

The problem types differed in the statements that followed. The first version, the **Monty Hall Standard**, fully described the host's protocol:

> "First you point toward a door," he says. "Then I'll open one of the other doors to reveal a goat. After I've shown you the goat, you make your final choice whether to stick with your **initial** choice of doors, or to switch to the remaining door. You win whatever is behind that door." You begin by pointing to door number 1. The host shows you that door number 3 has a goat.

2   P. Mueser and D. Granberg, "The Monty Hall Dilemma revisited: Understanding the interaction of problem definition and decision making," University of Missouri, unpublished paper.

Although this is not exactly the version that is most common in the literature, it makes unambiguous the assumptions that are necessary for justifying why switching is the best choice. Given this protocol, the chance of winning for someone who sticks with door 1 is 1/3, while the chances of winning for someone who switches to door 2 are 2/3.

The second version, called **Monty Hall Ambiguous**, does not specify the host's protocol, but merely indicates one instance of it:

> You begin by pointing to door number 1. The host shows you that door number 3 has a goat. He says to you, "Now that I've shown you the goat, you can make your final choice whether to stick with door 1 or switch to door 2."

This corresponds closely to the version of the Monty Hall Dilemma as it is commonly, and incorrectly, stated. In order to calculate whether it is best to switch, some assumptions must be made about the host's protocol. If a contestant follows a strategy of sticking with the original choice, the chance of winning is 1/3—assuming the position of the prize cannot be changed to take into account the contestant's choice. On the other hand, a strategy of switching can yield a probability of winning that can vary all the way from 0 to 1, depending on the host's protocol. In this version, the host's motives could play an important role in determining the outcome.

The third version of the problem, called **Monty Hall Random** fully specifies the host's protocol as one in which he chooses randomly among all three doors but, in this particular case, has opened door 3:

> "First you point toward a door," he says. "Then I'll open one of the three doors at random. After that, you make your final choice whether to stick with your initial choice of doors, or to switch to one of the other doors. You win whatever is behind that door." You begin by pointing to door number 1. The host shows you that door number 3 has a goat.

Here the chance of winning is 1/2 for sticking with door 1, and 1/2 for switching to door 2. The rational contestant should be indifferent between sticking and switching in this third version, Monty Hall Random.

If the subjects were to solve the problem on a rational basis, they would be indifferent between switching and sticking when facing the Monty Hall Random problem. Their response to the Monty Hall Ambiguous problem would depend on assumptions about the host's protocol. It was not fully specified, so any answer could be justified.

The results indicate that the decisions to stick or switch did not vary significantly according to which instructional condition the subjects read. People leaned toward sticking rather than switching in all three conditions. In this study, 19% (10/54) chose switch in the Monty Hall Standard, 18% (10/56) chose switch in the Monty Hall Random, and 11% (6/53) chose switch in the Monty Hall Ambiguous condition. Thus, subjects in the ambiguous condition did not respond in a way that was significantly different from subjects in the standard or random condition. Also, there is no indication in their choices that subjects can distinguish meaningfully between the standard and random versions, even though these two conditions clearly imply a different response on rational grounds.

Gambling, Risk and Uncertainty

Subjects seem, in fact, more inclined to respond to this as a general type of situation involving a two stage decision. They may see it as a quasi-competitive situation in which the host and his allies are competing against the contestant for the acquisition or retention of scarce resources. It is presented as a game, and the word game implies competition, particularly in an American setting.

There is also the element of a gambling situation. Perhaps most gamblers have heard that the casinos love a big winner for the favorable publicity generated by such an event. In the same sense, people on a game show might think it would be bad publicity if no one ever won a car on the game show. In that event the public would lose interest and turn their attention elsewhere. Yet the host appears as the competitor, and his knowledge might be envied. "If only I knew what he knows, I could easily win a car."

There is a distinction that may prove helpful in accounting for the general tendency observed in this chapter for people to stick with a preliminary decision, whether it be in the Monty Hall or Roulette Dilemma, and whether it involves a standard, ambiguous or random protocol for the host. The distinction is between **risk** and **uncertainty**. The delineation between these two was made by John Maynard Keynes and Frank Knight working independently.[3]

Risk is inherent in decisions in which the probabilities associated with various outcomes can be calculated. Playing the game of the roulette wheel at a gambling casino involves risk, as do many card games. The probabilities can be calculated rather precisely in such a case.

Uncertainty is involved in decisions in which the probabilities of various outcomes are not known and cannot be calculated. Playing the stock market is an example of a situation in which people make judgments under conditions of great uncertainty.

Leroy and Singell attempted to explain the distinction between risk and uncertainty in terms of conventional decision theory. Risk, they suggested, involved circumstances in which probabilities could be estimated independently of a decision maker's action, while uncertainty involved circumstances where the very choice by the decision maker would interact with the probabilities of various outcomes.[4]

Viewed in these terms, play against an opponent often involves uncertainty, as in poker. In the Monty Hall Dilemma, the host may be viewed by the contestant as an opponent or adversary. If the Monty Hall Dilemma is viewed as involving such play, this may, in part, explain the difficulty that both statistical professionals and the lay public display in their attempts to estimate appropriate probabilities. Subjects facing the standard version of the Monty Hall or Roulette Dilemma act as they would in the face of

---

3   F. Knight and J. McClure (ed.), **Risk, Uncertainty, and Profit**, 2009, Kissimmee, FL: Signalman.

4   S. Leroy and L. Singell, "Knight on risk and uncertainty," **Journal of Political Economy**, 1987, **95**, No. 2, 394-406.

uncertainty because they are unable to interpret the significance of the host's protocol, although, formally what they face is risk. Their decisions suggest that while people have learned, at a superficial level, to play such games, they usually have little facility in calculating the true probabilities. Part of the explanation of our subjects' choice behavior then comes down to this distinction. They play the game as if it were one involving uncertainty, when, in fact, it is of the type involving risk.

CHAPTER 7
A CROSS-CULTURAL COMPARISON

The Desirability of a Cross-Cultural Comparison

The initial empirical studies of people's reactions to the Monty Hall Dilemma used letters written to Marilyn vos Savant and the responses of undergraduate students at the University of Missouri to word problem surveys and laboratory experiments. While the letter writers are an interesting lot, they are self-selected from an unrepresentative sample. The unrepresentative sample consists of people with access to **PARADE** magazine. Of those with access, only a certain unknown percentage read the column, "Ask Marilyn." Of those who read the column on a given date, only a certain unknown percentage reacted strongly enough to go to the trouble of composing a letter and getting it sent.

While analysis of the letters can be revealing of how some people think about the Monty Hall Dilemma, the letter writers cannot be considered representative of **PARADE** magazine readers, much less the U.S. population as a whole. Even this would beg the question of how representative people in the U.S. are of humanity in general.

Thus, Marilyn vos Savant was technically in error when she summarized the responses she had been receiving regarding her analysis of the Monty Hall Dilemma, "Overall, nine out of ten **readers** completely disagree with my reply (emphasis added)." Mark Glickman, a statistician at Harvard University, wrote to her to point this out:

> If a reader agrees with your solution, the chance the reader will respond is small since there is no apparent controversy. On the other hand, if a reader does not agree with your solution, there will be a greater inclination to write in and express this sentiment.

The point, of course, is that vos Savant would have been on much firmer ground if she had said 9 out of 10 letter writers instead of 9 out of 10 readers.

Much the same can be said of the unrepresentativeness of the undergraduates at the University of Missouri. One difference, however, is that they were not self-selected participants. They knew very little about what they were getting into when they agreed to participate in a survey or a computer-administered experiment. These undergraduates comprised what is often called an "availability sample."

Within the social and behavioral sciences there are different concerns. On the whole, sociologists and political scientists are more concerned with getting a representative or random sample of some population in order to be able to draw valid inferences about the nature of things in the population. Social psychologists and psychologists generally are much less concerned with random sampling and more concerned with randomly assigning people to different conditions in order to observe the effect of some experimentally manipulated variation.

Overall, these features reflect differential concern over problems of external validity (generalizability) and internal validity. The orientation of social psychologists has implicitly been, "Let's take care of internal validity first and worry about external validity later." Here I want to merely point out this difference rather than argue about the merits and hazards of one approach compared to the other. But it would be agreed that the very best scientific approach for the social sciences would involve both random selection of subjects and random assignment to different experimental conditions. Moreover, when we say random selection of subjects, we would be speaking (ideally) of a random selection of human beings, not just U.S. adults alive in a given year.

Of course, the research we do, including that reported in this book, generally falls well short of the ideal. Nonetheless, the ideal is something to keep in mind even though in practice we often have to settle for "half a loaf." With this as background it seemed natural to wonder how generalizable the results of the initial Monty Hall studies were. I distinctly recall discussing with Thad Brown how it might be that people from certain cultures or subcultures could respond differently; but that was only speculation on our part, albeit interesting and stimulating.[1]

In this chapter, I report data from a cross-cultural comparison of responses to two-stage decision problems involving conditional probability. These problems are the "notorious" Monty Hall Dilemma and the Russian Roulette Dilemma. In both of these dilemmas, the subject chooses whether to stick with an initial decision after receiving some valid information about the unchosen alternatives. To the U.S. subjects tested in the initial Monty Hall studies, the rational solution (switch and win with 2/3 probability) seemed highly counterintuitive. Consequently, they showed a strong tendency to stick when they should have switched.

This raised a question that can only be addressed through cross-cultural comparisons. Is there something inherent in the intersection between human cognition and the Monty Hall Dilemma itself, which leads people generally to stick in this two-stage decision when they should switch? Or is there something specific to the socialization process in the U.S. which leads people reared in the U.S. to respond predominantly in a non-optimal way to the Monty Hall Dilemma?

This way of framing the research question parallels that used by Marshall Segall, Donald Campbell, and Melville Herskovits in their research on the susceptibility of people in various cultures to optical

---

1   Thad's view was that the Mujahideen in Afghanistan would be an interesting group to study.

illusions.[2] They referred to the question as the "nativist-empiricist controversy." The "nativist" perspective presumed that people perceive optical illusions a certain way because of their native endowment as human beings, and therefore, predicted similarities across cultures. The "empiricist" orientation presumed that people learn from being socialized in a particular type of environment how to perceive, and therefore, predicted differences due to varying learning experiences.

The Monty Hall Dilemma can be considered a cognitive illusion in that the odds appear to be 50:50, when, in fact, they are 2:1. While the subjects in the initial U.S. studies showed a strong and significant tendency to stick in the Monty Hall Dilemma, there were, nonetheless, indications that the situation is at least somewhat fluid. Although a sizable majority (80-90%) decided to stick in their first encounter with the Monty Hall Dilemma, the tendency was certainly not invariant as some subjects did decide to switch. A further indication of fluidity is provided by Gilovich, Medvec, and Chen, who showed that a confident and assertive confederate can successfully influence a subject to switch (or stick) in the Monty Hall Dilemma.[3] This fluidity implies that how a cross-cultural comparison of responses to the Monty Hall Dilemma would turn out was by no means a foregone conclusion.

Part of the difficulty some people have with problems involving conditional probability has to do with ambiguity in the way the question is stated. Therefore, in devising the wording for the Monty Hall Dilemma in the present study, an effort was made **to minimize** ambiguity and to build into the wording certain key assumptions. For the 2/3 solution to obtain in the Monty Hall Dilemma, it is necessary to assume, as has been emphasized previously, that the host knows both the location of the prize and the subject's initial guess, and uses that knowledge to deliberately show an incorrect, unchosen alternative after the subject has made her initial

---

2   M. Segall et al., **The Influence of Culture on Visual Perception**, 1966, Indianapolis: Bobbs-Merrill.

3   T. Gilovich et al., "Commission, omission, and dissonance reduction: Coping with regret in the 'Monty Hall' problem," **Personality and Social Psychology Bulletin**, 1995, **21**, No. 2, 182-190.

guess. It is further assumed that the host is committed to the procedure of opening an unchosen, incorrect door, and to giving the contestant the choice of whether to stick or switch. Without evidence to the contrary, it is also reasonable to assume that the three doors are initially equally likely to contain the prize, and that when the subject's initial guess is correct, the host chooses randomly which of the other two doors to open.

Insofar as possible, these crucial assumptions were built into the wording of the Monty Hall problem used in this research. They were also kept in mind as the problem was translated into Chinese, Portuguese, and Swedish and then back translated into English prior to use in the cross-cultural phase of the study.[4] The goal in this exploratory study was to have about 200 undergraduate students, divided about equally by gender, in each of four countries think about and respond to a Monty Hall type of problem.

As a further comparison, within each country, about half of the subjects responded to the standard Monty Hall Dilemma, while the other half responded to an inverted form of the problem called the "Russian Roulette Dilemma" or Roulette Dilemma. In the Roulette Dilemma, there is a valuable prize behind each of two doors, and there is only one losing door. The subject selects a door, and then the host opens and eliminates one of the other doors which had been a potential winner. The subject is then given the choice of sticking with her initial selection or switching to the other remaining door.

Although the Monty Hall and Roulette Dilemmas are similar in structure and sequence, nonetheless, they are drastically different. The rational solution in the Monty Hall Dilemma is to switch in the final stage, while in the Roulette Dilemma the rational solution is to stick with one's initial guess. In either case, following the rational solution yields a 2/3 chance of winning.

The four countries (Brazil, China, Sweden, U.S.) were chosen on the basis of the author's available contacts. However, any fair-minded person would agree that the variance among these cultures is very substantial.

---

4 Brazilian, Chinese, and Swedish versions of the questions are available from the author, email: granbergd@missouri.edu.

The research was considered exploratory so no directional predictions were made. Some of the comparisons are of obvious interest. For instance, it is known that students in China do much better on a variety of mathematics tests than students in the U.S., even when intelligence is carefully controlled.[5] However, it is not known whether such differences extend to problems involving conditional probability.

Gathering the Data.

The U.S. data were gathered in undergraduate sociology and social psychology classes at the University of Missouri with 83 men and 107 women subjects. The Swedish data were collected as part of a survey of first year students in the departments of political science, journalism, and public administration at Göteborg University. This Swedish sample was comprised of 160 men and 186 women. The respondents in China were 136 students at East China Normal University and 63 students at Fudan University. The Chinese subjects were all first year students, averaging 18 years of age; these 99 men and 100 women were majoring in a variety of academic disciplines. The Brazilian sample was slightly older, averaging 21 years of age, and was evenly divided among social science, commerce, philosophy, and psychology majors. This sample of 200 consisted of half men and half women students.

In each country about one half of the students was randomly assigned to answer a form containing the Monty Hall Dilemma; the other half was given a form containing the Roulette Dilemma. Overall, 472 subjects in four countries answered the Monty Hall version and 463 subjects answered the Roulette version. Because the exact wording in these studies is important, the wording for the two dilemmas is given here in full. First, the wording for the Monty Hall Dilemma was as follows:

> Suppose you are a contestant on a game show. The host, who is known to be completely honest, has placed a new car behind one

---

5   D. Geary, "Reflections of evolution and culture in children's cognition: Implications for mathematical development and instruction," **American Psychologist**, 1995, **50**, No. 1, 24-37.

of three doors and a goat behind each of the other doors. "First you point to a door," the host says. "Then I'll open one of the other doors and show that it has a goat. After I've shown you the goat, you make your final choice, and you win whatever is behind that door." You begin by pointing to a door, say door number 2. The host then shows you that door 1 has a goat. What would your final choice be? Would you stick with door 2 or switch to door 3?

The wording for the Roulette version was as follows:

Suppose you are a contestant on a game show. The host, who is known to be completely honest, has placed a new car behind each of two of three doors and a goat behind the other door. "First you point to a door," the host says. "Then I'll open one of the other doors and show that it has a car. That door will no longer be available to you. After I've shown you that door with a car, you make your final choice, and you win whatever is behind that door." You begin by pointing to a door, say door number 2. The host then shows you that door 1 has a car. What would your final choice be? Would you stick with door 2 or switch to door 3?

What People Chose

The main results for this cross-cultural comparison are summarized as follows. In each country people responded similarly to the Monty Hall Dilemma by showing a strong tendency toward the non-optimal answer of sticking with their initial selection. The overall percentage of subjects who checked stick in the Monty Hall Dilemma was 83%, and ranged only between 79% for China and 87% for Brazil. The U.S. and Sweden were intermediate with 84% and 83%, respectively, checking that they would stick. These four percentages are not significantly different from one another. However, within each country, the observed split departed significantly from a 50-50 distribution. The 50-50 distribution is what one might expect if people did not have a propensity one way or the other or if they answered in a haphazard manner.

Similar results were found for the Roulette Dilemma. On this problem, for which the optimal solution is to stick, the overall percentage sticking was 84%, 78% for Brazil, 81% for China, 85% for the U.S., and 87% for Sweden. Once again, the four countries were not significantly different from each other, but the subjects within each country showed a significant departure from a chance distribution of 50-50.

Within each country, the responses to the Monty Hall Dilemma were not significantly different from those for the Roulette Dilemma. The largest difference occurred in the case of Brazilian subjects, 87% of whom chose to stick in the Monty Hall Dilemma, compared to 78% in the Roulette Dilemma. This difference is in the opposite direction from rationality, but even this difference of 9 percentage points is not statistically significant. Thus, people within each of these four rather different cultures showed a strong tendency to stick when they should stick but also tended to stick when they should have switched.

Combining across cultures and across the type of problem, women were more likely to indicate stick (86%) than were men (81%). Thus, this main effect of gender implies a slight and marginally significant tendency for women to stick more in two-stage decisions than men. However, this difference did not occur consistently across conditions or across cultures. In the Brazil-Monty and the U.S.-Monty conditions, women were significantly more likely to answer stick, but in the other six conditions, the gender difference was not statistically significant.

Interpreting the Results

The gender effect we observed was no more than a slight difference, and it is not easy to replicate. A safe way to put it is to say that if there is a difference, women may be ever so slightly more likely to stick with an initial judgment in a two-stage decision. However, the difference is so small that it does not warrant much attention.

Our main finding is of cross-cultural similarity in the tendency of people to respond erroneously to the Monty Hall type of two-stage decision problem. In other words, the results imply support for the nativist as opposed to the empiricist perspective. Of course, as with any inductive type of problem, the very next culture that would be examined could provide contradictory evidence.

Nonetheless, thus far it appears that there is something inherent in the Monty Hall Dilemma, as a cognitive illusion, which leads people in very different cultures to respond similarly. People misapprehend the true probabilities, perceiving the odds to be even, and then tend to stick with their original selection. They are probably seeking to avoid the greater negative affect associated with being wrong after switching away from the winning alternative. Because the four cultures studied encompass very considerable variety, the temptation is to infer that the tendency to stick in the Monty Hall Dilemma reflects a universal human propensity. However, it would be premature to go that far.

It can also be argued that while the wording was made as nearly the same as feasible, the meaning of the problem posed as a hypothetical may have been quite different. That is, people may have been responding similarly but for different reasons. In retrospect, perhaps the problem should have concerned some valuable prize other than a new car. It is difficult to say exactly what meaning the problem had for the Chinese students, living in a country with fewer televisions and cars per capita and to whom the game show format may have been relatively unfamiliar. However, that would create more of an interpretive problem if the Chinese students had responded differently, but they did not. The game show format is highly familiar in the other countries, Brazil, Sweden, and, of course, the U.S. where the show, "Let's Make a Deal," with Monty Hall as host, originated.

Another objection concerns what motivation or incentive the subjects had to do well, i.e., to solve the problem correctly. However, evidence from laboratory experiments using a Monty Hall type of problem with real monetary incentives implies that the tendency to stick with a preliminary, revocable decision observed in the four cultures in the current study does not exaggerate what would be observed if real prizes were at stake. Also, the fact that people in each culture departed significantly from a 50-50 distribution of responses is a strong indication that these subjects were giving their best estimate of what they would actually do and were not responding randomly.

People in any culture can, of course, learn to solve conditional probability problems successfully—even though they are not easy. Such problems often involve counterintuitive solutions and cannot be solved correctly by merely applying everyday common sense. This type of problem can be referred to as a biological-secondary task, using the terminology of David Geary. Therefore, one would predict greater success for a given culture only if that type of problem were emphasized and practiced in schools or elsewhere in that culture.[5]

CHAPTER 8

THE NUMBER OF DOORS

An Abstract Analysis

In her very first attempt to explain the Monty Hall Dilemma, vos Savant resorted to the clever device of expanding the number of doors. The implication is that this makes the correct answer blatantly obvious. But does it?

Increasing the number of doors from 3 to 1,000,000 has the advantage of changing the odds, making them much more "one-sided," while the correct answer remains the same (switch). Granted the usual but necessary assumptions, the probability of winning by sticking when there are 3 doors is 1/3, compared to a probability of 2/3 for switching away from one's first guess. With a million doors, the probability of winning by sticking is reduced to only .000001, but one can be nearly certain (probability = .999999) of winning by switching. By framing her analysis in this way, the implication was that by expanding the number of doors from three to a million, the correct solution of switching would become more obvious and, therefore, more compelling.

In a similar vein, William Martin, Chairman of the Department of Nuclear Engineering at the University of Michigan, suggested expanding the problem to one hundred doors with a goat behind each of 99 doors and a car behind the other door. The host would deliberately show 98 goats after the contestant's initial guess. Martin reported using the Monty Hall problem to introduce students to Monte Carlo methods while teaching the "Statistical Simulation of Complex Physical Systems."[1]

Writing in the **American Statistician**, Steve Selvin gave a formula, which he credited to David Ferguson, (N-1)/[N(N-n-1)].[2] This formula yields the probability of winning by switching where N is the number of doors and n is the number of incorrect doors shown after the contestant has made an initial pick. Ferguson's formula is a very general one that can cover any dilemma in which there is one prize, any number of doors, and any number of incorrect doors shown by the host. If we limit ourselves to those situations in which the host opens all but one incorrect door, leaving a choice between only two doors in the final selection, the formula can be simplified somewhat farther. In that case, the probability of winning by sticking is 1/N, and the probability of winning by switching is the reciprocal 1-(1/N) where N is the number of doors.

Figure 8.1 shows the results of an application of Ferguson's formula. When all but one incorrect door, i.e., N-2 incorrect doors are shown, the advantage of switching increases as the number of doors increases. On the other hand, if only one incorrect door is shown, the advantage of switching decreases as the number of doors increases. If the lines in Figure 8.1 were extended, they would never reach 1.0 or 0.0. There is always the possibility, admittedly remote, when there are many doors, that one's original guess was the winner. Thus, the advantage of switching never reaches 1.0. Similarly, when there are many doors and the host opens only one, there is at least a small advantage to switching. Where there are only three doors, showing all but one incorrect door and showing one incorrect door are the same thing. But as can be seen in Figure 8.1, the two lines begin to depart drastically when the number of doors reaches four and beyond.

---

1   W. Martin, unpublished letter to Marilyn vos Savant.

2   S. Selvin, "On the Monty Hall problem," **American Statistician**, 1975, **29**, No. 3, 134.

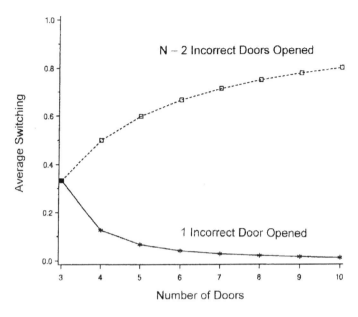

Figure 8.1. Relative advantage of switching in the MHD as a function of the number of doors (N) when only 1 or N – 2 doors (all but 1 incorrect doors) are opened.

The implication of vos Savant and Martin is that if only people would expand the number of alternatives in the Monty Hall Dilemma, they would then get it right. That hypothesis, however, lends itself nicely to an empirical test or a series of tests. Rather than speculating idly about what people should do or would probably do, let us examine in a forthright manner what people actually do.

Some Empirical Data

In one of our laboratory experiments, we manipulated the number of doors and the number of incorrect doors shown after the subject's initial guess. In the baseline condition of that experiment, in which there were three doors and one incorrect door shown, 11% (10/87) decided to switch on their first encounter with the Monty Hall Dilemma. In a second condition, there were five doors and three incorrect doors were shown after the subject's initial guess. In that condition, in which the probabilities of winning by sticking and switching were .20 and .80, respectively, 13% (6/47) switched on their first try at the Monty Hall Dilemma. In the third condition, there were seven doors and five incorrect doors were shown after the subject's initial guess. In that condition, the percentage who switched on their first Monty Hall trial decreased back to 11% (5/45). The difference among these three conditions on trial 1 was not significant. Therefore, there is a basis for doubting the efficacy of simply expanding the number of doors as a way of getting people to see the advantage of switching in the Monty Hall Dilemma.

This result, interesting though it may be, deserves to be qualified in at least two ways. First, since we did not expand the number of doors in that experiment beyond seven, we cannot extrapolate with confidence beyond that level. That is, the experiment which has just been described cannot tell us what people would do if there were 50, 100, 1,000 or 1,000,000 doors. Admittedly, it might be a bit hard for people to visualize a million doors, just as it is probably difficult for people to truly comprehend their remote chance of winning a lottery. However, they could probably visualize 50 or 100 doors, e.g., as in a hotel, without great difficulty. Second, the only part of the experiment with 3, 5, and 7 doors that has been described thus far is what people did on the very first trial. It is quite possible that the manipulation would have an effect on later trials, i.e., on the speed and the success with which they learned to switch, even though it had no effect on the initial trial.

In regard to the first of these qualifications, an experiment was done subsequently by Marcia Wisdom on the campus of Missouri Valley College. She used a one-trial word problem, varying the form to which people were randomly assigned to respond. The independent variable was whether the scenario described involved a standard 3 door condition or a condition with 100 doors. The wording for the 3 door condition was as follows:

> Suppose you are a contestant on a game show. The host, who is known to be completely honest, has placed a new car behind one of the three doors and a goat behind each of the other two doors. "First you point to a door," the host says. "Then I'll open one of the remaining doors and show that it has a goat. After I've shown you the goat, you make your final choice, and you win whatever is behind that door." You begin by pointing to a door, say door number 2. The host then opens door 1 and shows that it has a goat. What would your final choice be? Would you stick with door 2 or switch to door 3?

The wording for the 100 door condition was similar, but expanded the number of doors so that a new car was behind one of the 100 doors and a goat behind each of the other 99 doors.

> "First you point to a door," the host says. "Then I'll open all but one of the remaining doors to show you that each of them has a goat. After I've shown you the goats, you make your final choice, and you win whatever is behind that door." You begin by pointing to a door, say door number 26. The host then opens all but doors 26 and 57 and shows that they have goats. What would your final choice be? Would you stick with door number 26 or would you switch to door number 57?

The results of this experiment were that in the 3 door condition, 85% (200/234) indicated they would stick, compared to 75% (172/229) in the 100 door condition. This difference of 10 percentage points is statistically significant, indicating that the difference in wording regarding the number of doors had some effect. However, it is also fair to observe that most of the people in the 100 door condition opted to stick and only about a fourth of them marked switch.

We should also take note of a potentially interesting gender difference in that study. In the standard 3 door condition, 84% (92/109) of the women and 86% (105/122) of the men indicated they would stick with their initial guess, practically no difference. However, in the 100 door condition, 86% (78/91) of the women and 68% (94/138) of the men marked that they would stick. In other words, in the 100 door condition men (32%) were more than twice as likely as women (14%) to indicate they would switch. This interaction effect reveals a reliable difference, one that is statistically significant.

We now return to the laboratory experiment in which people played the Monty Hall Dilemma when there were 3, 5, or 7 doors and the host (the computer) opened all but one of the incorrect doors after the subject's initial guess. We described previously what happened on the very first trial, but the experiment did not end there. Rather the subjects were shown the result of the first trial, and then the dilemma was repeated until each subject had played the game for 50 trials. Subjects were told about a prize of $25 for those who were among the best.

Table 8.1 presents results of switching in the various conditions, dividing the 50 trials into 5 blocks of 10 trials each. In the standard baseline condition with 3 doors, subjects increased their switching from 11% on trial 1 to 38% on trials 1-10 combined, and 59% on trials 41-50. In the 5 door condition in which the host opened 3 incorrect doors after the subject's initial guess, the subjects switched 13% on trial 1 but then increased their switching to 43% on trials 1-10 and finishing the series with 76% switching on trials 41-50. The corresponding percentages for the 7 doorshow 5 condition were 11% for trial 1, 53% for trials 1-10 and 87% for trials 41-50. Clearly, these three conditions yielded very different results. Adding more doors, while continuing to show all but one incorrect doors, seemed to have no effect on the initial reaction, but facilitated greatly the learning that took place across time.

Table 8.1

*Average Number of Switches (0-10) on Five Blocks of 10 Trials in the Five
Conditions in the Monty Hall Dilemma*

Experimental condition		Trials				
Number of doors	Number of incorrect doors shown	1-10	11-20	21-30	31-40	41-50
7	1	3.8_{ab}	4.8_a	4.8_a	5.4_a	4.9_{ab}
5	1	3.4_{ab}	4.6_a	5.0_a	4.9_a	4.7_a
3	1	3.2_a	4.2_a	4.6_a	5.1_a	5.9_b
5	3	4.3_b	6.9_b	7.5_b	7.4_b	7.6_c
7	5	5.3_c	7.0_b	7.3_b	8.3_b	8.7_d

Note: In each block of 10 trials, reading down, averages with a subscript in common are
not significantly different by a Duncan multiple range test.

The preceding percentages are based on the proportion of second-stage
decisions in which the subject decided to switch at that point along the way.
For instance, on trials 31-40, the 47 subjects in the 5 door-show 3 condition
made 470 judgments. Of those 470 judgments, 348 were to switch (74%).
Another way of analyzing the same data is to ask what percentage of the
subjects in a given condition completely mastered the problem. Our working
definition of complete mastery, admittedly a strict standard, was to switch
on each of the last 10 trials. By this standard, only 9% in the baseline 3-door
condition had mastered the problem completely, as evidenced by their switching on each trial in the fifth block of trials (41-50). This compares with 28%
in the 5 door-show 3 condition and 44% in the 7 door-show 5 condition.

The latter percentage can be viewed two ways. On the bright side, it
is evidence of human learning and constitutes a very substantial improvement over the baseline condition. On the other hand, it is also true that
even when the odds favor switching by 6:1, a majority (56%) still have not
mastered the problem after playing it for 50 trials.

Partly for the sake of symmetry, but also out of curiosity, we included two additional conditions in the laboratory experiment involving the number of doors. Those conditions used 5 doors or 7 doors, but only 1 incorrect door was shown following the subject's initial guess. In these conditions, there is still some advantage in switching, but the advantage is much less than in the baseline 3 door condition.

The results for the 5 door-show 1 and the 7 door-show 1 were not significantly different from the baseline condition. The percentage switching in the 5 door-show 1 condition was 19% (9/48) on trial 1, 34% on trials 1-10, and 47% on trials 41-50. The corresponding percentage switching for the 7 door-show 1 condition were 25% (11/44) for trial 1, 38% for trials 1-10, and 49% for trials 41-50. The percentage of subjects showing complete mastery of the problem by switching on each of the last 10 trials was only 6% for the 5 door-show 1 condition and 5% for the 7 door-show 1 condition. These percentages are not significantly different from each other or from the 9% who mastered the problem in the baseline 3 door condition.

To summarize, the number of doors manipulation in the laboratory experiment had no effect on a person's initial propensity to stick or switch in the Monty Hall Dilemma. On the other hand, the number of doors manipulation had a strong effect on learning to switch over the entire series of 50 trials. The asymmetry of the effect may also be informative. Making the solution more unambiguous (comparing 3 doors-show 1 with 5 doors-show 3 and 7 doors-show 5) increases switching and mastery of the problem very substantially. However, making the solution more ambiguous (comparing 3 doors-show 1 with 5 doors-show 1 and 7 doors-show 1) had no effect. This asymmetry implies that one reason it is difficult to learn through direct experience, that the best solution is to always switch in the standard 3 door Monty Hall Dilemma, is that the relative advantage of switching is not sufficiently compelling.

It may be objected that while the subjects in the 7 door-show 5 condition learned to switch a lot, and many of them appeared to have mastered the problem, it is still possible that they didn't fully understand the problem or the reasons that switching conferred a sizable advantage. If they did, the knowledge would presumably transfer successfully to some comparable but different situations. There are many ways such a transfer effect could be examined.

Based on the results of the number of doors laboratory experiment, we had reason to doubt that a person's initial propensity to stick when one should switch in the Monty Hall Dilemma is reduced by making the objective odds more compelling than 2:1. However, that doubt is reduced by the word problem study by Marcia Wisdom, comparing a standard 3 door Monty Hall Dilemma with a 100 door-show 98 condition. She found the tendency to stick was reduced significantly by expanding the number of doors to 100. However, it will be recalled that the differential effect seemed to occur only among men respondents. A future word problem study could compare the 3 door condition with other conditions involving 10, 100, and 1,000 doors.

After we had completed these studies, we encountered two related studies dealing with the number of doors. Page reported a one trial experiment with three conditions. In the standard 3 doors condition 12% (2/17) switched, compared to 47% (8/17) in a 10 doors condition, and 87% in a 100 doors condition (14/16) switching.[3] We are in agreement on the direction of the finding, but our results for the 100 doors condition were much weaker. Part of the difference between these experiments may be due to the incentive of possibly winning $5 in Page's study while the Missouri Valley College students received no such reward. Also, Page's subjects were Business Graduate Students at an elite institution, Northwestern University, who had all completed a course on probability theory.

The second recent paper, retrieved via the Internet, reported two studies in which the number of doors was the independent variable.[4] The first compared Williams College students in two conditions. In the 3 "box" standard Monty Hall condition, only 6% (1/16) gave a switch response,

3 S. Page, "Let's make a deal," **Economic Letters**, 1998, **61**, No. 4, 175-180.

4 T. Ben-Zeev, J. Stibel, M. Dennis, and S. Sloman, "Increasing working memory demands improves probabilistic choice but not judgment on the Monty Hall Dilemma." Unpublished paper.

compared to 50% (8/16) in a 100 box condition. In their second study, carried out with 152 Brown University Undergraduates, the number of boxes was varied at six levels (5, 6, 7, 8, 9, 10). The corresponding percentage switching was 10, 20, 23, 47, 45, and 58. Thus, the effect they obtained was quite strong with an almost consistent linear effect. The largest difference between adjacent conditions occurred between boxes 7 and 8. It will be interesting to see if that difference can be replicated.

In any event, the number of doors variable does have an effect. The questions that remain concern the strength of the effect and the shape of the function.

CHAPTER 9

THE NUMBER OF PLAYERS

In the previous chapter, we considered what happens when the number of doors in the Monty Hall Dilemma is expanded beyond three. That related to the first way Marilyn vos Savant tried to explain the "switch and win with 2/3 probability" solution. She did so by asking the reader to imagine a million doors, 999,999 of them containing goats and the one containing a new car. Many of her letter writers took up that theme.

A few of the people who wrote letters to vos Savant regarding the Monty Hall Dilemma asked the interesting question of what happens if we expand the number of players. As we shall see, they did so mainly as a device to question or refute her solution.

This is not something we have done in any of our experiments, except in the two-person team study to be described in the illusion of control chapter 12. Therefore, I shall use a few letters to illustrate this argument, and then go on to discuss a genuine paradox involving the number of players. It is worth discussing because it shows how some people think about the problem and how they analyze and dissect it.

We begin with a brief letter sent in response to Marilyn vos Savant's second column about the Monty Hall Dilemma:

December 3, 1990

Dear Marilyn:

Considering the following: You choose door #1. I, as a co-contestant choose door #2. The host opens door #3 and reveals a goat. According to your theory, you and I would both be advised to switch our door choices to increase our chance of winning. This would set up a paradox where we would both gain an advantage by switching our choices, which of course can not be. Enclosed please find an ace and two jokers.

Yours truly,

F.I., Traverse City, Michigan

A few years later, I read this letter while doing a content analysis of Marilyn's mail, and I wrote the following response to Mr. F.I. I explained who I was, what I was doing, and inquired as to whether he had any further thoughts on the matter. To refresh his memory, I enclosed a copy of Marilyn's first two columns on the subject together with a copy of Steve Selvin's two letters in the 1975 volume of the **American Statistician** which first formulated the problem and offered a solution.

My letter of July 6, 1993, continued:

> The problem you pose in your letter is a fascinating erstwhile paradox, but in fact it involves an extension which fundamentally alters the structure of the situation by reducing the degrees of freedom of the host to zero. Let me explain. If there are three doors with one winner and two losers, following an initial selection by a lone guest, the host can always **knowingly** open one of the other doors which is a loser. The key here, and it is one that is neglected in your letter, is the basis on which the door to open is selected after the initial choice. If the host knows the correct answer and the initial guess, knowingly opens a losing door, and then gives the guest the choice of whether to stick with the initial selection or switch to the remaining

door, the chances of winning by switching are 2 in 3, and the chance of winning by sticking is 1 in 3. On the other hand, if the host chooses a door to open randomly or without knowledge of the location of the winner or the initial guess, then the chance of winning is 1 in 2 regardless of whether the guest decides to stick or switch.

Getting back to the problem you posed, let's see what happens if we increase the number of doors from 3 to 4 so that the host retains a degree of freedom: 4 doors, 1 winner placed randomly behind door A, B, C, or D. I choose A. You choose B. Taking these choices into account as well as knowing which door is the winner, the host opens a losing door, D. Now you and I have to decide whether to stick with our initial, respective, choice or switch to C. The probability for A, B, C, and D being correct initially was .25. The chances of C or D being correct initially was .50. No matter what you and I chose initially, the host could always **knowingly** open an unchosen, incorrect door; therefore, doing so does not change the probability of our initial selection being correct; that remains at .25 for each of us. D having been knowingly eliminated, the probabilities are now .25 for A, .25 for B, and .50 for C. If I stick with A or switch to B, my probability of winning is .25, but if I switch to C, my probability of winning is .50. On the other hand, if the host had in ignorance chosen a door to open by some random process, and just happened to open D which just happened to be a loser, then the probability of each door being correct is 1/3 and I gain no advantage by sticking with A or by switching to B or C.

So the problem you posed modified radically the one Marilyn was addressing by eliminating the host's degree of freedom. Marilyn was basically correct and stimulated a lot of people to think about a problem in probability—the solution to which is counterintuitive, and not easy to derive or learn.

If you have any reactions to this letter or to the enclosed materials, I would be pleased to hear from you.
Cordially,
Donald Granberg

That was the end of my correspondence with F.I. A somewhat longer letter, involving essentially the same extension of the number of players, was received from a professor of mathematics. Strongly worded, it also was written shortly after Marilyn's second column on the Monty Hall Dilemma appeared in print. To avoid the possibility of taking part of it out of context, I quote the letter in full:

December 3, 1990

Dear Ms. vos Savant:

It is apparent from your "Ask Marilyn" column, dealing with probabilities, which appeared in the December 2, 1990, issue of **PARADE Magazine**, that being smart is no guarantee of being correct. Your analysis of the game-show probabilities, and the analogy involving the pea under a shell, reveals a misunderstanding of the rudiments of probability theory, and an appalling lack of logic.

Let me preface my discussion of the faults in your arguments by a general comment about probability theory. The probabilities that we assign to a set of future events are a measure of our ignorance. As we gain information about one event of the set, the probabilities that we assign to **each** of the events will change. For example, if we learn that one of the set of events has a probability of zero, the remaining probabilities must increase. Note that the game-show host would assign very different probabilities to the choices of the contestant than would the contestant him/her self, because the host knows what is behind the doors, whereas the contestant does not. As the contestant's knowledge of specific events increases, the entire set of probabilities changes.

Consider first the shell game, in which a single pea is placed under one of three shells. Let's label the shells A, B and C and suppose that one player, named Abe, puts his finger on shell A and a second player, named Ben, puts his finger on shell B. In the absence of any information of the location of the pea (other than the facts that there is only one pea and it is under one of the three shells), we assign a value of 1/3 to the probability of the pea being under

117

any one shell: $pA=pB=pC=1/3$. (Note that the probabilities must sum to 1.) Now suppose that shell C is lifted and the pea is not seen. We now know that $pC=0$. According to your argument, now $pA=1/3$ and $pB=2/3$ because "nothing has been learned to allow us to revise the odds" on the shell under Abe's finger. But by the same reasoning, pB should remain 1/3! Now either $1/3 + 1/3 = 1$ or your argument is wrong. I leave it to you to figure out which.

Turning now to the game show. Your explanation involving the list of six possibilities has two errors of logic when applied to the stated problem. First, we know from the statement of the problem that two of these (having an auto behind door 3) **do not occur**, and therefore **cannot be used** to determine the probabilities. Barring these two possibilities, switching to door 2 does not improve the contestant's odds. Second, if we do allow these possibilities (having an auto behind door 3) but restrict the contestant to switching to door 2 as stated in the problem, the third possibility you list leads to a **loss,** not to a win. Again switching does not improve the contestant's odds.

Let's revise the game show slightly by supposing that there are two contestants: Abe who chooses door 1 and Ben who chooses door 2. After a goat is found behind door 3, by your logic each candidate would increase his probability of success from 1/2 to 2/3 by switching his choice with the other contestant. Again, either 2/3 +2/3 = 1, or else your argument is wrong.

I urge you to lower your mantle of omniscience and (following the lead of Ann Landers) seek the advice of experts when the subject matter is outside your area of expertise. Your ignorant responses are hurting the fight against mathematical illiteracy.
Sincerely,
D.L., Tallahassee, Florida

My letter and enclosures to Professor D.L. were essentially the same as my letter to F.I., as quoted above, so I won't repeat most of it. However, my letter to D.L. of July 6, 1993, concluded:

[S]o the choice you twice offered to Marilyn, "either 1/3 + 1/3 = 1 or your argument is wrong," is false in that your modification of the problem altered the situation radically by eliminating the host's degree of freedom. I do not agree that Marilyn's "analysis of the game-show probabilities, and the analogy involving the pea under a shell, reveals a misunderstanding of the rudiments of probability theory, and an appalling lack of logic." Nor do I believe that her "ignorant responses are hurting the fight against mathematical illiteracy." On the contrary, she was basically correct and stimulated a lot of people to think about a problem in probability—the solution to which is counterintuitive, and not easy to derive or learn. If you have any reactions to this letter or to the enclosed materials, I would be pleased to hear from you.

Sincerely,

Donald Granberg

In this case, I did receive a reply from D.L., but it was not the sort of acknowledgement I would have thought appropriate. He could have said, "I was wrong. There is a set of plausible circumstances or assumptions under which Marilyn's 2/3 solution is correct." Instead he wrote:

July 23, 1993

Dear Professor Granberg,

This is in response to your letter of July 6, 1993, concerning the three-door problem. Upon reflection (before receiving your letter), I have concluded that the problem is ill-posed; its solution is beyond the realm of probability. If the game-show host had not known which door concealed the prize, or if he had chosen which door to open by a flip of a coin, then the proper choice for the contestant could have been estimated by probability theory. However, since the game-show host knew what was behind the doors and deliberately chose one, we must know his motives for doing so in order to assess the proper course of action for the contestant.

For example, it may be that the contestant is the nephew of the show's producer, who had instructed the host to do what he could to ensure that his relative won the car, which was behind door #2. On the other hand, the show may have been over budget and the host had been instructed to get a winning contestant to change his choice from a winning door #1 to a losing door #2.

Since the agent of choice (the game-show host) has prior knowledge, probabilities have nothing to do with solving the problem. Sincerely, D.L.

D.L. is correct in asserting that under some circumstances, the host's motives could be important, especially if he is not following a fixed protocol. However, as pointed out in Chapter 1, we can specify a set of assumptions, none of which is implausible, under which the counterintuitive "switch and win with 2/3 probability" solution prevails. Assume a knowledgeable host, who knows both the location of the prize and the contestant's initial guess. Assume further that the host is committed to disclosing an unchosen, losing door after the contestant's initial guess and to giving the contestant the choice of whether to switch or stick. Finally, assume that when the contestant's initial pick is correct, the host chooses randomly which of the other two doors to open. These are the key assumptions that need to be built into the wording of the problem in order to reduce ambiguity. Under these circumstances, the contestant has only a 1/3 chance of winning by sticking with the initial decision but a probability of 2/3 of winning by switching. D.L.'s assertion that since the host has prior knowledge, "probabilities have nothing to do with solving the problem," is flat-out wrong. Furthermore, the host's motives are **irrelevant** when the host is following a fixed procedure—even though that procedure involves some randomness, e.g., in placing the prize behind one of the doors or in choosing which door to open when the contestant's initial pick is the winner. The 2/3 solution in the Monty Hall Dilemma works when the host is using a fixed protocol and has no discretion on what to do.

Thus far in this chapter we have considered how adding a second contestant choosing a different door fundamentally alters the situation in the Monty Hall Dilemma by eliminating the host's degree of freedom. Now I want to turn to an even more interesting and amazing development involving the expansion of the number of players. Suppose there are two contestants. The first (Anne) goes through all the steps in the customary way in the Monty Hall Dilemma. That is, she picks a door, say door 2. Then the host opens door 3 and shows it to be a loser. Anne knows what has transpired and is now free to choose to stick with door 2 or switch to the only other remaining door 1. As is well known by now, she could win either way but her chances are twice as good by switching (2/3) as they are by sticking (1/3).

Now suppose at this point we bring on a second contestant (Beth) who knows nothing about what has happened on stage. All Beth knows is that there are two doors, numbered 1 and 2, and that one of them contains a valuable prize, and she is supposed to guess which door contains the prize. For Beth, who lacks the knowledge that Anne has, the doors are equally likely to contain the prize and, therefore, each has for her a probability of .50.

This paradox in probability was introduced in a more colorful way by Marilyn vos Savant in her third column on the Monty Hall Dilemma:

> The original answer (switch and win with 2/3 probability) is still correct, and the key to it lies in the question: **Should you switch?** Suppose we pause at that point, and a UFO settles down onto the stage. A little green woman emerges, and the host asks her to point to one of the two unopened doors. The chances that **she'll** randomly choose the one with the prize are 1/2. But that's because she lacks the advantage the original contestant had—the help of the host.

Given her description, we could call this the **Martian Paradox**. What is so paradoxical about this is that the same arrangement of two doors has different probabilities for different people as a function of their different experience and knowledge.[1] For the contestant who knows what door she picked originally, and what door was subsequently eliminated by the host, the probability of winning can be 2/3 if she decides to switch. For the Martian who came on the scene when there were only two alternatives left and is not informed about what has happened, the two doors are equally likely at .50 to contain the prize. R.H. Good, a physicist at California State University, Hayward, wrote an insightful letter about many facets of the Monty Hall Dilemma, including this one. He concluded that it "seems almost as paradoxical as quantum mechanics."

---

1   One of the anonymous reviewers asked this insightful question, "Would the Martian Paradox be predicted by Bayes Theorem because of the role of prior knowledge." My response was, "Of course it would. Why didn't I think of that?"

CHAPTER 10
THE NUMBER OF STAGES

In the standard three door Monty Hall Dilemma, there are two stages to the decision, the initial pick followed by the decision to stick with it or switch to the only other remaining alternative after the host has shown an incorrect door. An intriguing extension of the basic Monty Hall Dilemma has been provided by M. Bhaskara Rao of the Department of Statistics at North Dakota State University.[1] He analyzed what happens when the dilemma is extended beyond two stages. The number of stages can be as many as the number of doors minus one. Thus, for example, a Monty Hall Dilemma with seven doors could have as many as six stages, the initial guess followed by five instances in which one additional losing door is eliminated in each succeeding stage. After each losing door is shown, the contestant gets the choice of sticking or switching.

Here is an example of how a three stage Monty Hall problem might be worded when there are four doors, one of which is the winner. The host says:

1   M. Bhaskara Rao, "Letter to Editor," **American Statistician**, August, 1992, **46**, No. 3, 241-242.

"You point to one of the doors, and then I will open one of the other doors to show a goat. Then you decide whether to stick with your initial pick or switch to one of the remaining doors. Then I will open another door (other than your current pick) to show a second goat. You will then make your final decision by sticking with the door picked on the previous round or by switching to the only other remaining door."

Now there are three stages instead of the usual two and four different strategies for the contestant. She can stick with her initial guess both times, switch both times, switch and then stick, or stick and then switch. Table 10.1 shows these four strategies as well as the probability of winning associated with each of them.

Table 10.1

Probabilities of Winning with Four Strategies in a Three Stage Monty Hall Dilemma

Stage	1	2	3	Probability of Winning
	Pick	Stick	Stick	.250
	Pick	Switch	Stick	.375
	Pick	Stick	Switch	.750
	Pick	Switch	Switch	.625

People who accept the correctness of the 2/3 solution in the standard Monty Hall Dilemma might presume that one does best by switching in both Stage 2 and Stage 3. However, as shown in Table 10.1, the counter-intuitive solution to the three-stage Monty Hall Dilemma is to stick in Stage 2 and then switch in Stage 3. These remarkable probabilities were published by Rao in the **American Statistician**, and have been verified by Ken Mueller, a student assisting me, using computer simulation. The solution can also be shown by enumeration of all the possible combinations and calculating the corresponding probabilities.[2]

As you think about it, consider that, in two of the cases, stick-stick and stick-switch, the probabilities are the same as they would be in a two stage, four door Monty Hall Dilemma. That is, if you are going to stick with your initial guess regardless, it doesn't really matter if the host shows you the two incorrect doors one at a time or both at once. Therefore, the probability of winning by sticking in both stages 2 and 3 with four doors is .25. Similarly, the probability of winning by following the stick and then switch strategy is the same (.75) as if the host had skipped the second stage and simply opened two incorrect doors prior to the final choice.

The underlying principle is that in a multi-stage Monty Hall Dilemma, the optimal strategy is to stick with one's initial hunch until the very last chance and **then** switch.[3] For instance, suppose there are 10 doors, and following your initial guess, the host opens an incorrect, unchosen door and offers you the chance to switch eight times. The first seven chances to switch, you should say, "No thanks," but to the last offer to switch, you should say, "Yes, I think I will." Psychologically, it would seem to be very hard to follow such a strategy. The momentum seems to be building favorably in relation to your initial guess. Unfortunately, so far as I know, no one has yet attempted to study systematically how people actually choose in a multi-stage Monty Hall Dilemma.

---

2   V.V. Bapeswara Rao and M. Bhaskara Rao, "A Three-Door Game Show and Some of its Variants," **Mathematical Scientist**, 1992, **17**, No. 2, 89-94.

3   This version of the Monty Hall dilemma is referred to by Jason Rosenhouse as "Progressive Monty." See Chapter 4 in **The Monty Hall Problem: The Remarkable Story of Math's Most Contentious Brain Teaser**. J. Rosenhouse, 2009, New York: Oxford University Press.

CHAPTER 11

COUNTERFACTUAL REASONING

The results of the early Monty Hall Dilemma research implied that for solving two-stage decision problems, the human brain is not well equipped to process conditional information. Rather than being objective and efficient information processors, like a computer, humans may be "wired" to choose conservatively. We may tend to stick with a tentative selection, even when there is no rational basis for that selection, and when it would be perfectly rational to switch to another alternative.

In the Monty Hall Dilemma, the first reason why people stick when they should switch is that they err in deriving the relevant probabilities. They usually think the second stage involves a 50:50 situation when, in fact, the odds are 2:1. But then the question becomes, why do people overwhelmingly tend to stick in the face of what appears to be a balanced situation in which they think they have a 1/2 chance of winning by sticking and a 1/2 chance of winning by switching? Even if the true probability were .50 for winning by sticking, there would be no rational basis for sticking. If people flipped a coin in their minds to decide, one would expect 50% switching or something approximating that level. But by now we know that is not the case.

One possibility is that people may be engaging in **counterfactual reasoning.** Counterfactual thinking is defined as "an imagined alternative to an actual event."[1] Historians and social scientists often ask questions that prompt people to think in this way. For instance, one very common question is, "How might the war in Vietnam have developed differently if President John Kennedy had not been assassinated in Dallas in 1963?" There is no really thoroughly convincing answer to such a question, but it is a way of stimulating people to think about the causes of events.

At a more mundane level, social psychologists have used vignettes like the following:

> After entering a local grocery store, John hears a commotion behind him. Turning, he discovers that the person entering immediately after him is being congratulated and awarded cash and prizes for being the one millionth person to enter the store.[2]

How must John feel about this? Regretful? Frustrated? Angry? Perhaps, but he may also be stimulated to think counterfactually, and that, in turn, may cause him to experience certain emotions. John might imagine this counterfactual scenario through the process called mental simulation.

> As John was about to enter the grocery store, he stopped to open the door for the person behind him, and in doing so, John himself became the one millionth person to enter the store and thus was showered with cash and prizes.[3]

In commenting on their choices, some subjects in the first word problem experiment described in Chapter 6 showed evidence of counterfactual thinking. For instance, four of the subjects volunteered these thoughts when asked the basis for their decision:

---

1   F. Gleicher et al. "The role of counterfactual thinking in judgments of affect," **Personality and Social Psychology Bulletin**, 1990, **16**, No. 2, 284-295.
2   Ibid.
3   Ibid.

"I wouldn't want to pick the other door because if I was wrong I would be more pissed off than if I stayed with the 2nd door and lost."

"Never change an answer because if you do and you get it wrong it is a much worse feeling."

"It was my first instinctive choice and if I was wrong, oh well. But if I switched and was wrong it would be that much worse."

"I would really regret it if I switched and lost. It's best to stay with your first choice."

Subjects in the number of doors word problem experiment in Chapter 8 similarly showed signs of reasoning counterfactually. Here are a few examples of comments made by subjects who decided to stick in that study:

"(I would stick) just because of the fact that it had worked so far, and if I were to change and be wrong it would be twice as bad."

"(I would stick) because if I changed my mind and went with door 57 and there was a car behind 26 I would never forgive myself. I try to go with my first choice if I don't have any other evidence to prove I might be wrong."

"There is just as good a chance of there being a goat behind 57 as there is one being behind 26. I don't like to second guess myself."

"I have a better chance of winning if I go with my first choice. If I'm wrong, no big deal, but if I change or switch to Door 57 it'll irritate me that I didn't go with my original judgment."

"(I'd) stay with my first answer. Too much thought can cause confusion."

"Because when you answer something, then change that answer, 9 times out of 10 your change was for the worse."

"Because I would rather be wrong from the start and stick with it than switch and have been right in the first place."

"Why not? If I switch to door #3 I might regret it."

"Because if you change and it is behind Door 2 you will regret it and usually most prizes are in the middle."

"Staying with your first instinct can cause you less worries and regret."

It appeared from the comments made by these people in the word problem studies, in response to open-ended questioning, that they were indeed using counterfactual reasoning. It was as if they were asking themselves via mental simulation, "How would I feel if I switched and lost? How would I feel if I decided to stick and lost?" Of course, on logical grounds it is equally relevant to ask, "How would I feel if I switched and won? How would I feel if I decided to stick and won?" However, in their answers people seemed to dwell more on the two former questions than on the two latter ones.

From the comments volunteered by the people in these word problem studies, it was as if they thought there would be more negative affect (feelings) associated with losing after switching than with losing after sticking. In both of these cases, the subject has lost, but psychologically the situations may still be different. People who switch and are then incorrect may feel especially badly because they had the winning alternative correctly identified at first but then switched away from it. In essence, they had it made but then let it go. People who stick and are incorrect at least know they never had the correct answer "in their grasp."

Yet one can go only so far with anecdotal evidence. Therefore, a study was designed to test this counterfactual thinking hypothesis. Students in undergraduate classes completed a questionnaire that contained a description of the standard Monty Hall Dilemma similar to that used in the word problem experiments in earlier chapters. In this study, however, instead of asking people what they would choose to do, they were randomly assigned to a scenario in which they had decided to stick and lost (N=56) or one in which they had decided to switch and lost (N=55). The wording in the former, following the standard description of the Monty Hall Dilemma, was as follows:

129

You begin by pointing to door number 2. The host then shows you that door 1 has a goat. You decide to stick with door 2 rather than switching to door 3. The host then shows you that door 2 has a goat and door 3 has the new car. Thus, you DO NOT WIN the new car.

The wording for the switch and lose subjects was the same for sentences 1, 2, and 5. The third and fourth sentences were, "You decide to switch to door 3 rather than sticking with door 2. The host then shows you that door 3 has a goat and door 2 has the new car." Subjects in both conditions were then asked, "How do you think you would feel at this point?" They then made a series of ratings by putting a check mark somewhere on eight lines to indicate how they thought they would feel. Only the ends of the lines were labeled, for example, "Not at all surprised" and "Completely surprised."

On two of the scales the differences between the two conditions were statistically significant. People in the switch-and-lose condition thought they would feel more frustrated and angry than people in the stick-and-lose condition. Subjects in the switch-and-lose condition also thought they would be feeling less happy, less fortunate, more disappointed, and more upset, but the differences on these scales were not statistically significant. These data, even though they involve a hypothetical vignette, provide some support for the counterfactual interpretation of why people are reluctant to switch in the Monty Hall Dilemma.

It is of interest that it was the term frustration which most successfully differentiated the two conditions. Frustration has been defined in psychology as the experience of having one's progress toward a goal thwarted or blocked. The goal in this case is to win a new car. Somehow the procedure of guessing, being shown an incorrect, unchosen alternative by the host, and then switching one's guess to a losing door must conjure up feelings of considerable frustration in people's minds.

A counterfactual approach suggests that in arriving at their final decision in the Monty Hall Dilemma, people may use the cognitive heuristic of mental simulation. That is, they may ask themselves questions about how they would feel with various outcomes. Generally, it is thought by social psychologists that counterfactual thinking and affect are greater when a negative situation involves action rather than inaction.[4] In the Monty Hall Dilemma, switching would involve an action and sticking could represent inaction.

Positive outcomes are thought to be less likely to stimulate counterfactual thinking. For instance, a person who wins a race may be less likely to spontaneously think, "If I hadn't trained so hard, I would not have won," than a person who loses a race is to think, "If I had trained harder, perhaps I could have won."

If this principle applied equally to favorable and unfavorable outcomes, then it would explain the preference to stick rather than switch only if one assumed that people want to avoid situations high in affect. But perhaps the principle applies more to negative than to positive outcomes, and people may be trying to avoid the very negative affect associated with losing after switching. "Damn, I had the right answer but changed it" is a common expression of anguish familiar to teachers using multiple choice tests. The study described in this chapter supported the counterfactual hypothesis that people avoid switching in the Monty Hall Dilemma, in part, because they anticipate they would feel worse if they switched and lost than if they decided to stick and then lost.[5]

---

4 J. Landman, "Regret and elation following action and inaction," **Personality and Social Psychology Bulletin**, 1987, **13**, No. 4, 524-536.

5 For an in-depth analysis of counterfactual reasoning as it pertains to the Monty Hall Dilemma, see J.V. Petrocelli and A.K. Harris, "Learning inhibition in the Monty Hall Problem: The role of dysfunctional counterfactual prescriptions," **Personality and Social Psychology Bulletin**, 2011, **37**, No. 10, 1297-1311.

CHAPTER 12
THE ILLUSION OF CONTROL

One possible reason why people are reluctant to switch in the Monty Hall Dilemma is the **illusion of control**. This is a social psychological concept which relates two levels of reality, the social and the psychological. The term illusion in psychology has been used most extensively in the study of perception. (See Chapter 2.) This harkens us back to the very beginnings of experimental psychology which grew out of the philosophical concern over the relationship between mind and matter.

How do variations in the physical world correspond to changes in our psyches, i.e., our experiences? This type of concern led to the development of psychophysics. As a light gradually becomes brighter, from some starting point how much brighter physically must the light become before the change is detected in our perceptions? An illusion occurs when there is a discrepancy or contradiction between physical and psychological reality. Railroad tracks may appear to converge on the horizon, yet we know it can't be true. Rather it is the "Ponzo Illusion."

In the same sense that instances of physical reality differ on some physical dimensions, e.g., weight, texture, brightness, so also social situations differ in dimensions such as the extent to which the outcome is under the control of the individual. I decide whether to interrupt a lecture. I decide whether to wear a seatbelt and whether to recycle beverage cans. This is not to say that such behaviors are immune from social influence, or that they are independent of the social context, but rather that they are of the sort that is generally thought to be under the volitional control of the person.

On the other hand, being subject to a draft lottery, and getting a "good" or "bad" number in that lottery, is almost entirely out of the control of the individual citizen. One may wish to be taller or shorter in height, but there is precious little one can do about it. Many college freshmen are assigned roommates by a process they do not understand and over which they have virtually no control. Being selected as part of a random sample of U. S. adults for a social survey is generally not within the control of the average citizen.

An illusion of control occurs when people sense that they have more control over their own fate than is actually the case. People selling in the numbers racket usually allowed their customers to select their own numbers, thereby giving them a sense of greater control than if they were arbitrarily assigned a number. The opposite perhaps also occurs, i.e., people having more control over what happens than they realize. For example, student evaluations of a faculty member's performance may be taken much more seriously in the process of considering faculty for tenure and promotion than the students filling out the forms ever imagined. In either case, there is an illusion, but the illusion of control concept refers specifically to the situation in which people implicitly think they exert more control than is actually the case.

Dice players appear to behave as if they had some control over the outcome of a toss. They may throw harder when desiring a high number and softer when wanting a low number. They may even believe that concentration and effort may influence the outcome, which is, in fact, a matter of good or bad luck. In an experiment, people bet more prior to the dice being thrown than after the dice were thrown but before the outcome was revealed.

Ellen Langer, who developed the illusion of control concept, made a basic distinction between skill-oriented and luck-oriented tasks.[1] One

---

1   E. Langer, "The illusion of control," **Journal of Personality and Social Psychology**, 1975, **32**, No. 2, 311-328.

can practice and improve one's performance in skill-oriented tasks such as chess or billiards. Similarly, one can practice luck-oriented tasks such as keno or roulette, but one's performance does not improve accordingly. Langer theorized that an illusion of control is more likely to occur when a luck-oriented task, such as a lottery, has features that are normally associated with skill-oriented tasks.[2] Specifically, she singled out choice, familiarity, involvement, and competition as such features. By manipulating these factors she was able to show that confidence in one's winning at a chance-oriented event increased when people were given choices, when the alternatives were familiar, when people were more involved, and when they were competing. People choosing their lottery tickets are reluctant to trade them in, and may demand an exorbitant price if someone else proposes to buy the lottery ticket they have chosen.[3]

So in this chapter we consider another possible reason why people are reluctant to switch in the Monty Hall Dilemma even after they have concluded erroneously that it is a 50-50 proposition. Specifically, we are pursuing the possibility that an illusion of control may be involved. Generally speaking, based on the foregoing discussion, the illusion of control may be considered a cognitive bias in which people have an exaggerated sense of influencing events in their own favor through their own actions.

When people make the initial selection in the Monty Hall Dilemma, this very act of choosing may create an illusion of control in their minds that causes them to be reluctant to abandon that choice. Note that this is despite the fact that they had no rational basis for that choice in the first place.

That describes what is alleged to occur in the standard Monty Hall Dilemma. Therefore, for comparison purposes, it is necessary to create a condition in which the illusion of control would be less likely, i.e., an

---

2   E. Langer and J. Roth, "Heads I win, tails it's chance: The illusion of control as a function of the sequence of outcomes in a purely chance task," **Journal of Personality and Social Psychology**, 1975, **32**, No. 6, 951-955.

3   M. Bar-Hillel and E. Neter, "Why are people reluctant to exchange lottery tickets?" **Journal of Personality and Social Psychology**, 1996, **70**, No. 1, 17-27.

"anti-illusion of control" condition. We did this by taking the initial choice out of the hands of the participant. The initial selection is made by another person, the person's partner, and the subject makes only the second-stage decision to stick or switch. This parallels rather closely how the illusion of control concept has been operationalized in prior research. The hypothesis was that switching will occur more often in the two-person condition, both on the first encounter with the dilemma and in the process of learning across trials.

Subjects and Procedure for the Illusion of Control Experiment

Participants in this experiment were 145 undergraduate students (88 women and 57 men) at the University of Missouri. The experimenter began a program named LUMAD (Let Us Make A Deal). Subjects were randomly assigned by the computer to either the standard Monty Hall (control) condition or the "anti-illusion of control" (experimental) condition. Subjects in the standard condition were given the usual instructions.

The instructions for the experimental ("anti-illusion of control") condition began the same, but departed at a certain point to create the two-person condition. In the two-person condition, participants read that the decision would be divided into two parts, the initial guess to be made by one person and the final decision to be made by another person. In fact, the first decision was made by the computer choosing a door at random, and the subject was always assigned to make the final decision. People in the two-person condition read these instructions:

> In this condition, each part of the decision will be made by a different person. By random assignment, it was determined that you will be making the one with an X in front:
> a. the FIRST initial stage of the decision
> X b. the SECOND final stage of the decision
> Thus, in your case, the first stage of each decision will be made by another person working at another computer terminal linked to this one. The final decision will be made by you.

On each trial, subjects were shown the three doors. People in the standard condition were asked to make an initial guess. In the two-person condition, people were told the other person's initial guess. In both conditions, people were then shown that one of the unchosen alternatives was incorrect. In the standard condition, people were told, "You picked Door 3. For your information the ACE is not behind Door 1. Press 2 or 3 for the second and final guess." (The door numbers are just an example.) In the two-person condition, the name **Rhonda** or **Randy** was substituted for the word **You**. After each second-stage decision, the content of the doors was displayed, and the message read, "Congratulations, Door 2 is correct. You have won one point." or "Sorry, but the ACE was behind Door 3." This same procedure was followed for 50 trials in each condition.

Results of the Illusion of Control Experiment

As predicted by the illusion of control hypothesis, people in the two person condition were significantly more likely to switch on trial 1 (38%, 25/66) than people in the standard condition (9%, 7/79). Of course, in the standard condition, people were tending to stay with a choice they had made themselves. In the two-person condition they were still tending to stay, albeit to a lesser extent, with a selection that had been made by another person, a stranger. In the case of the standard condition, the observed percentage departed very significantly from a 50-50 split, while in the two-person condition that result was more marginal.

Let us now jump ahead to see what the people in these two conditions did on the very last trial 50, after they had 49 trials to learn that it was in their interest to switch. On trial 50, subjects in the Monty Hall standard condition had increased switching to 48% (38/79). In the two-person condition, 56% (37/66) switched on trial 50. This difference of 8 percentage points is not significant. Thus, it appears that the two conditions started out quite differently on trial 1, but by trial 50 they were no longer significantly different. This is the first indication that the experimental manipulation of the illusion of control variable was having a significant effect, but one that was limited in duration.

The 50 trials were also divided into 5 blocks of 10 trials each. The percentage of switching in each condition on each of the 5 blocks of trials is given next.

There it is apparent that the biggest difference occurred on the initial block of trials, i.e., on trials 1-10. The percentage of trials on which subjects in the standard condition switched increased across the 5 blocks from 32% on block 1, 46% on block 2, 54% on block 3, 52% on block 4, and 55% on block 5. The corresponding percentages for the two-person condition were 50%, 53%, 52%, 54%, and 56% for blocks 1-5, respectively.

Thus, it is evident that the two conditions produced different trends. In the standard condition, switching started lower, increased significantly, and then leveled off at a plateau just over 50% switching. In the two-person condition, switching started at a higher level, but showed essentially no trend across trials. The difference between the two conditions was significant for blocks 1 and 2, but not for blocks 3, 4, and 5.

The percentage of subjects who mastered the problem completely by switching on all of the last 10 trials was relatively low for both conditions. Only 3% (2/79) of the people in the standard condition met this difficult criterion, compared to 11% (7/66) in the two-person condition.

In terms of how it is experienced by the subjects, we can ask what is the actual correlation between the number of times a person switched and the point total the person accumulated across the 50 trials. (The maximum possible range was 0-50 for both variables.) In the standard condition, that correlation was +.60, and in the two-person condition, it was +.56.

If we square these correlations and move the decimal point, we can estimate the percentage of the variance in point totals that can be explained by the amount of switching. That percentage is about 36% and 31% for the two conditions, respectively. The magnitude of these correlations is, of course, not fixed. Rather, they could be lower if there was less interpersonal variation in the amount of switching, or they could be higher if there was more interpersonal variation in the amount of switching.

Additional Evidence for the Illusion of Control

In the preceding chapter, evidence was presented that was consistent with the idea that counterfactual thinking is one reason why people tend to stick with their initial decision in the Monty Hall Dilemma. In this chapter, an experiment was described which purported to show that the tendency to stick is due to an illusion of control. Well, which is it? It could be that both factors are operating. The tendency to stick is pronounced enough that it could have more than one cause. That is, there may not be just a single reason why people are reluctant to switch in the Monty Hall Dilemma.

The experiment reported in this chapter supported the illusion of control interpretation in some important ways. People making the stick or switch decision after the initial guess had been made by another person apparently felt more free to switch. People who made the initial guess themselves may have experienced an illusion of control and, therefore, became more reluctant to switch. Yet this apparently liberating effect of having the initial guess made by another person did not prove advantageous in the long run. On trials 21-50, the standard Monty Hall condition and the two-person condition produced switching at about the same rate.

Thus, our anti-illusion of control manipulation had a significant effect in the predicted direction, but the effect was short lived and did not really facilitate long range learning of the correct solution to the Monty Hall Dilemma. In effect, the anti-illusion of control manipulation enabled people to get to the plateau of switching slightly more than 50% of the time sooner, but it did not make it more likely that the correct solution of always switching would eventually be discovered.

The manipulation in this experiment was intended as a direct test of the illusion of control hypothesis rather than a critical experiment testing between competing explanations. The significant differences in the opening trial and in trials 1-20 corroborate the illusion of control hypothesis concerning why people tend to stick in the early trials of the Monty Hall Dilemma, but they are probably not sufficient to rule out other possibilities.

Before getting to the other possibilities, let us consider one more bit of evidence which provides some additional support for the illusion of control interpretation. In a survey, 323 undergraduate students answered this question:

> Out of a studio audience of 450 people, you and two other people are chosen by a random and completely fair process to have a chance to win a car. The car has been placed by using a table of random numbers behind Door A, Door B, or Door C. No door will be opened until each person has a door. In order that no two people choose the same door, the person choosing first gets to pick any of the three doors, the person choosing second gets to pick one of the two remaining doors, and the third person gets to have the one remaining door. To decide the order of choosing, the host gives each person $100. That hundred dollars can be used to bid for the right to choose first or second, or you can choose to keep all hundred dollars and not bid at all.
>
> What would you do with the $100?
>
> I would bid $_____ (0 to 100) for the right to choose first and $_____ (0 to 100) for the right to choose second.
>
> Note: The sum of the numbers in the two blanks must not be larger than $100.

Given the wording as it was stated, the rational solution to the problem is to bid nothing and keep the $100. If the other people bid something, and get to choose first and second, the door that is left for you will have just as good a chance of containing the big prize. Choosing a door first or second may foster an illusion of control but would not increase the actual control or the chance of winning.

Would people be willing to give up some money for the illusion of control? It appears that many people indeed would. The respondents in this survey said they would make an average bid of $20.62 to choose first and $15.39 to choose second. Overall, 42% said they would bid some money to choose first or second. 8% said they would bid the maximum ($100) for the right to choose first.

For balance, it should be stated that in this case, the rational majority (58%) said they would not bid any money. Nonetheless, it is of interest that at least 2 of 5 respondents showed a potential tendency to behave irrationally. Apparently, many people are willing to commit resources for what they should have realized is no more than the illusion of control.

Other Possibilities

What are some of the possibilities other than the illusion of control? Here we shall mention four. It could be that people are less likely to engage in **counterfactual thinking** in the two-person experimental condition than in the standard condition. Consequently, they would be less motivated to avoid the negative affect associated with losing after switching in the two-person condition. Some social scientists have posited a general conservative preference called the **status quo bias**.[4] It is captured rather nicely in the cliché, "If it's not broke, don't fix it." That could be involved in the reluctance to switch in the standard Monty Hall Dilemma. When it comes time for that second stage decision, there has been nothing that has been shown to be wrong with the initial choice. However, if it were that simple, then people should be just as inclined to stay with the status quo, i.e., the initial decision, in our two person condition. That is, even when that initial decision has been made by another person, it still creates a status quo condition.

One could address the matter of how much it matters who created the status quo. In the present study, the first stage (tentative) decision was made by a stranger of the same sex as the subject named Rhonda or Randy. What if it had been one's mother or son or spouse who had made the initial decision, i.e., someone with whom one feels a greater degree of ego-involvement and attachment? Wouldn't this increase the reluctance to switch away from their initial preference? Or what if the initial selection had been made by one's rival or enemy? In short, the characteristics of the other person,

---

4 W. Samuelson and R. Zeckhauser, "Status quo bias in decision making," **Journal of Risk and Uncertainty**, 1988, **1**, No. 1, 7-59.

if known and the relationship established with the subject could certainly play an important role. Previous research has found that parents become as ego-involved in their children's performance as they would be in their own.[5]

Another concept from social psychology which may be relevant here is **belief perseverance**.[6] When people have formed a belief, e.g., that the death penalty does or does not deter the crime of murder, it is difficult to disabuse them of that belief. The typical experiment on belief perseverance draws people from a common pool of subjects. This ensures that they don't differ in their initial beliefs. Each person is randomly assigned to receive information supportive of a particular belief, e.g., high risk takers make effective firefighters or high risk takers make poor firefighters. Each side finds the information persuasive and convincing. Later, the experiment is explained to the subjects, and an effort is made to disabuse them of the belief that had been created in the experiment. The key finding is that even after this debriefing stage, the two sides still retain, to a significant degree, the beliefs that had been instilled in them earlier, albeit in a reduced degree. Thus, the beliefs tend to persevere.

In fact, we don't currently know the subjective probabilities that people may attach to the three doors in the lab experiments. It could be that people retain a 1/3, 1/3, 1/3 subjective probability for doors 1-3, even after they have made a preliminary guess that door 2 hides the prize. It could also be that the subjective belief that door 2 is the winner becomes greater than 1/3 after stating that as a preliminary selection.

Studies in the psychology of **commitment** established that one of the consequences of behaving in line with a belief is a strengthening of that belief in the sense that it becomes more resistant to attack.[7] I may have no more than a hunch that the prize is hidden in back of door 3, but when I

---

5   M. Sherif and C. Sherif, **Social Psychology**, 1969, New York: Harper and Row.

6   C. Anderson, M. Lepper, and L. Ross, "Perseverance of social theories: The role of explanation in the persistence of discredited information," **Journal of Personality and Social Psychology**, 1980, **39**, No. 6, 1037-1049.

7   C. Kiesler, **The Psychology of Commitment: Experiments Linking Behavior to Belief**, 1971, New York: Academic Press.

state door 3 as my preliminary guess, I am committed to it psychologically even though the rules indicate that I am free to switch to the other remaining door.

So there you have it. There are at least five concepts (counterfactual reasoning, illusion of control, status quo bias, belief perseverance, and commitment), drawn from social psychology, that may be of use in trying to account for why people are reluctant to switch when they should do so in the Monty Hall Dilemma. In one sense, it would be nice if one could design a grand experiment which would enable us to test among these possibilities and rule out four of them. However, as indicated earlier, these concepts are not mutually exclusive and it is more likely that more than one, and possibly all of them, will end up being regarded as relevant to the Monty Hall Dilemma. In closing this chapter, we return to the distinction Langer made between skill-oriented and luck-oriented tasks. The Monty Hall Dilemma resembles real life in one important respect. One's fate is determined, in part, by chance or luck, but also, in part, by skill, insight, and developing a shrewd strategy. One can maximize one's chances by choosing the optimal strategy of always switching. Even then, one is by no means guaranteed a win, since the remainder is determined by chance. Two people each following the optimal strategy may, in fact, obtain scores that are quite different.

CHAPTER 13
DOORS WITH UNEQUAL PROBABILITIES

One of the original assumptions in the Monty Hall Dilemma was that the winning prize would be placed behind the door on a random basis with each door having an equal chance of being the winner. This is a good starting point and may be the most reasonable assumption absent evidence to the contrary.

One of the letter writers alluded to a rumor that many people had learned inductively that switching was advantageous by simply watching the TV program, "Let's Make a Deal," over an extended period of time. That seems doubtful, especially given the relatively small advantage due to switching among three doors and the irregular procedure actually followed by the host, Monty Hall.

Another possibility is that participants and members of the audience could develop inductively the impression that the host favored one of the doors, i.e., that some door contained the winning prize more often than could reasonably be expected by chance. Suppose, by one means or another, that the three doors are known to have different probabilities of being the winner. As a hypothetical example, by watching the show regularly, a person might notice that door 1 is the winner 45% of the time, door 2 40% of the time, and door 3 only 15% of the time. Moreover, within these quotas, the placement for a given contestant lacks predictability.

Thus, one of the basic assumptions is violated, but suppose the other assumptions are still valid. That is, the knowledgeable host is committed to opening an unchosen, incorrect door after the contestant's initial guess, and to giving the contestant the option of sticking or switching. Also, when the contestant's initial guess is correct, the host chooses randomly, with equal probability, which incorrect door to display.

The contestant begins the process by picking door 1, the most likely alternative. The host, taking this into account together with his knowledge of where the car is, opens door 2 to reveal a goat and then allows the contestant to stick or switch.

Should the contestant breathe a sigh of relief since the second most likely alternative has been eliminated, and stick with door 1 which had the highest initial probability of being correct? Or should the contestant switch to what had been the least likely alternative, door 3? One solution is to switch to door 3 since it now has an unconditional probability of .55 of containing the prize, compared to .45 for the other remaining alternative, door 1. In this view, with a **knowledgeable** host selecting the unchosen door to open, it is as if an "iron curtain" descends around the first pick, so that the probability that had been associated with the incorrect door that is opened transfers entirely to the remaining alternative. By this reasoning, so long as the initial probability of door 1 having the car is less than .5, one should switch.

But wait! For this problem, there is an even **better** strategy for the contestant to follow, suggested to me by Craig Anderson. Assuming the contestant knows the probabilities given above and knows the procedure to be followed by the host, the contestant can maximize the likelihood of winning the car by first picking the **least** likely alternative, door 3, and then switching to the remaining alternative after door 1 or door 2 is opened to display a goat. In that way, one can have an unconditional probability of .85 of winning the car by switching. The efficacy of this solution becomes more apparent by imagining a situation in which one of the three doors is known to have no chance of being the winner. If the contestant chooses that door initially, and the host opens an unchosen, incorrect door, the contestant could then be certain of winning by switching. Anderson's solution seemed highly counterintuitive, and we expected that it would be very rare for an experimental participant to come up with it spontaneously.

In fact, this problem with doors that have unequal probabilities turns out to be even more complex. People writing letters to Marilyn about the three doors problem debated whether this was a problem involving conditional probability. But in the case of doors with equal probability, it does not matter whether one uses unconditional or conditional probability since the solution is the same. However, when the doors have unequal probabilities, e.g., .45, .40, and .15, one can use the additional information of which door is opened by the host to condition the probability. Given the choice, conditional probabilities should be used in this case since more information is utilized and thus, the uncertainty is further reduced. That is, the expected probability can be specified more precisely.

Let us follow the example given earlier. The contestant picks door 1, the host opens door 2, and the contestant then makes the final decision to stick with door 1 or switch to door 3. For convenience, let's call doors 1, 2, and 3, respectively, doors A, B, and C. Applying the Bayesian formula for conditional probability, we want to know the probability of winning by sticking with door A, given that the initial probabilities are known to be .45, .40, and .15 for doors A, B, and C, respectively, and given that the contestant picked door A initially and the host displayed a goat in door B. The answer is given by using the formula:

$$P(A|b) = \frac{P(b|A)\,P(A)}{P(b|A)\,P(A) + P(b|B)\,P(B) + P(b|C)\,P(C)}$$

$$P(A|b) = \frac{(.50)(.45)}{(.50)(.45) + (.00)(.40) + (1.00)(.15)} = \frac{.225}{.375} = .60$$

The way to read this formula is the conditional probability of A being correct, given that A was chosen and B was opened, P(A|b), is equal to the probability of B being opened if A was correct, P(b|A) times the initial probability of A being correct, P(A), over the denominator. The denominator is read similarly. Given the rules, there is no chance that B would be opened if B is the winner, P(b|B); and if A is chosen and C is the winner, the probability of B being opened by the host, P(b|C), is 1.0.

It becomes apparent that the answer to the question is .60. Similarly, the answer to the complementary question, the probability of C being correct, given that door A was chosen and B was opened, P(b|C), turns out to be .40. That is derived by using the same denominator as above, but changing the numerator, P(b|C) P(C), to .15. Dividing .15 by .375 yields the probability of .40.

It is highly doubtful that these conditional probabilities can be derived intuitively. The conditional probabilities that are generated by 12 possibilities are shown in Table 13.1. With these probabilities in hand, it is now apparent what one should do, given the **a priori** probabilities of .45, .40, and .15 for doors 1-3, respectively. If one picks door 1 initially, one should stick if the host opens door 2 but switch if the host opens door 3. Similarly, if one picks door 2, stick if door 1 is opened but switch if door 3 is opened. If one picks door 3 initially, it is better to switch regardless of which door is opened by the host.

Table 13.1

Applying the Bayesian Formula for Conditional Probability to the Problem of the Doors 1, 2, and 3 with Probabilities of .45, .40, and .15 Respectively

Initial Pick	Door Shown	P Win Stick	P Win Switch
1	2	.60	.40
1	3	.36	.64
2	1	.57	.43
2	3	.31	.69
3	1	.16	.84
3	2	.14	.86

There are two things worth noting here. Unlike the standard problem with the doors having equal probability, it is not necessarily always to one's advantage to switch when the doors have unequal probabilities. It depends upon, i.e., it is conditioned upon, which door one chose initially and which door is opened by the host. Yet, when all is said and done, Table 13.1 shows that Anderson's solution is still the **optimal** one: select the door with the lowest initial probability and then switch!

Some Experimental Data on Reactions to Unequal Probabilities

Throughout this book we are concerned with the dual questions of devising rational solutions to problems, i.e., the issue of what people should do, but also the corresponding question of what people actually do. In the experimental phase of this problem, the Monty Hall Dilemma we used was slightly more complicated, in one respect, than the situation discussed above. A dilemma was posed with four doors instead of three. This made it possible to have a neat progression of probabilities with door 1 having a probability of .1, door 2 a probability of .2, door 3 a probability of .3, and door 4 a probability of .4. In the control condition, each door had a probability of .25. Subjects were told these probabilities, and the computer program was adjusted accordingly so that the stated probabilities were correct. That is, unlike many experiments in social psychology, this experiment did not attempt to deceive the subjects in any way, shape or form.

Before getting to the results, let us discuss the dilemma once more in a further effort to clarify unconditional and conditional probability. Suppose there are four doors each with an initial probability of 1/4. The **unconditional** approach asks, what is my chance of winning if I decide in advance to switch regardless of which doors are opened by the host? Thus, I follow a sequence in which I choose a door, perhaps at random, and the host knowingly opens two incorrect doors. Then when given a choice of whether to stick or switch, I switch. In these circumstances, the probability that my initial guess was correct was 1/4, and my chances of winning by switching are 3/4.

The **conditional** approach asks more specifically, for example, what is my chance of winning, given that I chose door 2 initially, the host opened doors 1 and 3, showing them to be losers, and then gives me a choice of sticking with door 2 or switching to door 4? Each approach yields the same solution when the initial probability for each door was .25: switch and win with a probability of .75—provided that the crucial assumptions are valid.

As was stated in the previous section, when the initial probabilities are unequal, it becomes more rational to use conditional probabilities. Now assume we have a Monty Hall Dilemma with four doors, but the initial probabilities are unequal and are known to be .1, .2, .3, and .4 for doors 1 through 4, respectively. Applying Bayes' formula for conditional probability once more, it can be shown that if I choose door 4 initially, and the host then shows that doors 2 and 3 are losers, the rational solution is to stick with door 4. As Table 13.2 shows, the probability of winning by sticking is about .57, given that I chose door 4 initially and the host showed doors 2 and 3 to be losers. Table 13.2 shows all of the possible combinations of initial selections by the contestant and doors opened by the host. It must be noted here, once more for emphasis, that the calculations in Table 13.2 presume that when the person's first selection contains the prize, the host chooses randomly, with equal probability, which two of the remaining three doors to open.

Table 13.2

Unconditional and Conditional Probabilities of Winning by Sticking and Switching in a Four-Door Monty Hall Dilemma with Unequal Probabilities

Contestant Chooses door	Host Opens door	Unconditional probability of winning by:		Conditional probability of winning by:	
		Sticking	Switching	Sticking	Switching
1	2,3	0.1	0.9	0.077	0.923
1	2,4	0.1	0.9	0.100	0.900
1	3,4	0.1	0.9	0.143	0.857
2	1,3	0.2	0.8	0.143	0.857
2	1,4	0.2	0.8	0.182	0.818
2	3,4	0.2	0.8	0.400	0.600
3	1,2	0.3	0.7	0.200	0.800
3	1,4	0.3	0.7	0.333	0.667
3	2,4	0.3	0.7	0.500	0.500
4	1,2	0.4	0.6	0.308	0.692
4	1,3	0.4	0.6	0.400	0.600
4	2,3	0.4	0.6	0.571	0.429

Note: The initial probability of each door being the winner is 0.1 for door 1, 0.2 for door 2, 0.3 for door 3, and 0.4 for door 4. The formula for solving each conditional probability involves an application of the general Bayesian formula: for example, substituting A, B, C, and D for doors 1–4, respectively, the conditional probability of A being the winner, when the contestant initially picks A and the host opens doors b and d can be determined by the formula:

$$P(A|bd) = \frac{P(bd|A)P(A)}{P(bd|A)P(A) + P(bd|B)P(B) + P(bd|C)P(C) + P(bd|D)P(D)}$$

It is evident from Table 13.2 that when the four doors have unequal initial probabilities, a more precise estimate of one's prospects can be derived by conditioning the probability estimate specifically on which doors have been used in a given sequence. Table 13.2 shows that when using conditional probabilities, the chances of winning by sticking or switching are affected both by which door one selects initially and by which incorrect doors the host opens. Yet, it is also apparent that the optimal solution is

still to choose the least likely option available, door 1, and then switch away from it.

So in the case of the standard four door Monty Hall Dilemma with equal probabilities, the optimal solution is **relatively** simple (pick any door and then switch). But the result is such that it is only moderately obvious that one has found the optimal solution (winning odds = 3:1). The unequal probability version of the Monty Hall Dilemma being used here requires a more clever solution as optimal (pick door 1 and then switch). However, if one tries it, it becomes quite obvious that the optimal solution has been found (unconditional winning odds = 9:1).

This implies the hypothesis that insightful learning may be more likely to occur when the doors in the Monty Hall Dilemma have such unequal probabilities initially. To the extent that it occurs, learning in the equal probability Monty Hall Dilemma may be more gradual and incremental. Prior to carrying out this experiment, it was unknown what people would do when faced with an unequal probability Monty Hall Dilemma. Perhaps they would simply choose the most likely alternative and stick with it. In that way they would experience moderate success and they may have no way of coming to the realization that they could be doing much better.

Experimental Procedure

The experimental subjects were 192 undergraduate students at the University of Missouri, 75 men and 117 women. The subjects were assigned randomly by the computer to either the standard equal probability condition or the unequal probability condition. People were told that they would be asked to make a number of decisions, picking among four doors, and that on each of 60 trials the goal was to find the ace. The sequence to be followed was explained carefully, that is, they would pick a door, then be shown that two of the unchosen doors were incorrect (jokers), and then make a final decision for that trial, deciding whether to stick with their initial guess or switch to the other remaining door. The instructions also stated that there was no limit to the number of trials on which subjects could stick or switch.

The manipulation of equal or unequal probabilities was made explicit in the preliminary instructions, and the computer program adjusted the actual probabilities accordingly. People were told, "On every trial, each of the doors is equally likely to be the winner, i.e., to contain the ACE. Thus, throughout the 60 trials, the initial probability for each of the four doors being the winner is .25." Or, they were told, "On every trial, the doors are NOT equally likely to be the winner, i.e., to contain the ACE. Throughout each of the 60 trials, the initial probability of Door 1 being the winner is .10; for Door 2 the initial probability is .20; for Door 3 the initial probability is .30; and for Door 4 the initial probability is .40. These initial unequal probabilities will not change during the experiment."

So the experiment was basically administered by the computer, and subjects proceeded at their own pace through 60 trials of the four door Monty Hall Dilemma. After each trial subjects were shown the contents of all the doors and told whether their final choice for that trial was correct or not.

Experimental Results

We look first at what people did on the very first trial since this is indicative of their initial propensity in the situation, prior to any possibility of learning the solution through direct experience. Table 13.3 shows the results for trial 1. The 11% (9/84) switching in the equal probability (even) condition replicates quite closely the results in comparable studies.

Table 13.3

Trial 1 Results Showing Initial Propensities in the Equal and Unequal Probability Versions of the Monty Hall Dilemma

First guess was door:	Second guess was door:				
	One	Two	Three	Four	Total
Equal probability condition					
One	16	1	2	0	19
Two	1	25	0	1	27
Three	2	2	32	0	36
Four	0	0	0	2	2
Total	19	28	34	3	84
Unequal probability condition					
One	4	0	0	1	5
Two	0	10	1	0	11
Three	0	1	24	3	28
Four	0	1	1	62	64
Total	4	12	26	66	108

Note: Cell entries are frequency data, indicating the number of people following each of 16 patterns of choosing on trial1. In the upper table, each door had probability of 0.25. In the lower table, the probabilities were 0.1, 0.2, 0.3, and 0.4 for doors 1–4, respectively.

In the unequal probability (uneven) condition, there was actually slightly less switching on trial 1 (7%, 8/108). The most common response (57%) was to select the most probable alternative, door 4, and stick with it. The counterintuitive nature of the uneven problem is reflected most strongly in the fact that only 1 person out of 108 (1%) played the optimal solution on trial 1; that is, she selected the least likely alternative (door 1) and then switched away from it. Not to detract from her correct solution, it is fair to note that she did not use this optimal strategy again until trial 9 and used it only intermittently throughout the 60 trials despite the fact that she always won when she used it. Overall, she used the optimal solution on only 10 of the 60 trials, actually somewhat less than the overall average of 14.0 for people in the uneven condition. Because she made the optimal response on the very first trial, her record deserved a special look. However, it does not appear that she had a special insight at the outset on trial 1 or throughout the series of 60 trials.

It is relevant to consider that if 108 people in the uneven condition had, in two trials, chosen randomly among the four doors, about 7 of them (1/16) would have come up with the optimal solution by chance alone! People in the even condition also did much worse on trial 1 with only 11% employing the optimal strategy that provides a three in four chance of success. The very large differences between conditions on trial 1 indicate that the subjects were being attentive to, and were acting upon, the accurate probability information they were given prior to beginning the game.

That some learning occurred during the 60 trials can be illustrated simply by looking at what the subjects did on the very last trial, compared to the results from trial 1. In the even condition, 68% switched on trial 60; this is the optimal solution for that condition regardless of which door they selected initially; the increase of 57 percentage points (11% to 68%) is very substantial. Relatively speaking, they improved 64% of the maximum possibility they had for improvement (57/89).

On trial 60 in the uneven condition, 79% switched and 38% chose door 1 and then switched; the latter is the optimal solution. Here the improvement was 37 percentage points, also impressive evidence of substantial learning.

We can also impose a tougher standard for learning. We could say that if the person had truly mastered the problem, they would switch on each of the last 10 trials in the even condition and select door 1 and then switch on each of the last 10 trials in the uneven condition. By that admittedly difficult standard, 18% (15/84) in the even condition and 22% (24/108) in the uneven condition mastered the problem by following the optimal strategy on the final 10 trials. The difference between the two conditions on that criterion was not significant.

An overall picture of the trends across trials can be obtained by dividing the 60 trials into 6 blocks of 10 trials each. Figures 13.1 and 13.2 compare the experimental conditions on two different dependent variables.

First, with regard to the average number of optimal responses, the two conditions differed rather substantially.

Monty Hall Dilemma (four doors)

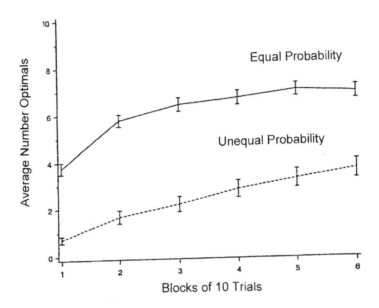

Figure 13.1. Average number of optimal solutions (± one S.E.) across 60 trials (six blocks of 10 trials each) in the four-door Monty Hall Dilemma with equal or unequal probabilities.

As shown in Figure 13.1, subjects in the even condition were at all points more likely to play the optimal response. However, there was a difference in the trend across trials. In the even condition, the percentage of optimal decisions (switch) increased significantly from block 1 to block 2 (from 37% to 57%). In the remaining blocks 3-6, there was no more than a slight increase, to 64% on block 3, 66% on block 4, 70% on block 5, and 68% on block 6. One could infer a negatively accelerated curve. That describes a situation in which a phenomenon shows a continuing increase, but the rate of increase is decreasing. Recall also that a significant minority (18%) of the subjects in the even condition was switching on each of the last 10 trials. This implies that the remaining 82% must have been in a more or less stalemate situation. It could be that they were **satisficing**, that is, settling for a level of winning that was satisfactory but not optimal. It may be that they didn't see how they could improve their chances of winning.

The subjects in the uneven condition also showed improvement over the first two blocks of trials, more than doubling from only 7% optimal on block 1 to 16% on block 2. However, they continued their improvement on blocks 3-6, going from 22% optimal on block 3, 28% on block 4, 32% on block 5 and 36% on block 6. So their record indicates slow but rather steady improvement, a more linear function.

Secondly, we consider the dependent variable of greatest interest to the subjects, the number of correct answers (the winning ace is found whether by sticking or switching). The results for the two conditions are shown in Figure 13.2. There it is evident that the subjects in the uneven condition did better at finding the ace on each block of 10 trials. If anything, their margin increased slightly on blocks 4-6. The percentage of correct guesses in the even condition began at 41% on block 1, and then increased to 53% on block 2, and then leveling off at 58%, 58%, 57%, and 58% for blocks 3 through 6, respectively. The percentage of correct guesses in the uneven condition was 49%, 57%, 61%, 68%, 69%, and 68% for blocks 1-6, respectively.

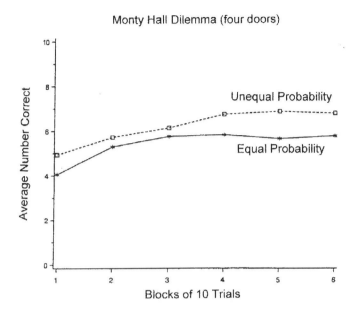

Figure 13.2. Average number of correct answers across 60 trials (six blocks of 10 trials each) in the four-door Monty Hall Dilemma with equal or unequal probabilities.

The results in Figure 13.2, pertaining to the number of correct answers, can also be considered in relation to what would be expected of hypothetical subjects following either a perfectly random or an optimal strategy. Overall, subjects in the even condition won on about 54% of the trials. This is substantially more than would be expected if they decided to stick on every trial (25%), only slightly more than if they decided to stick half the time and switch half the time (50%), and considerably less than the 75% success rate that could be expected if they had switched on every trial.

Subjects in the uneven condition won on about 62% of their trials, somewhat more than if they had consistently chosen the most probable alternative (door 4) and stuck with it (40%), but also considerably less than if they had consistently chosen door 1 and switched away from it (90%).

If we limit the analysis to the final 10 trials, after subjects had 50 trials to learn the optimal solution, subjects in the even condition won on 58% of the trials, which is 77% of what they could expect if they had played consistently the optimal strategy (58/75). In the uneven condition, subjects won on 68% of the final 10 trials, 76% of what would be expected from consistently playing the optimal strategy (68/90). One might assign an overall grade of C+ for the learning performance of these experimental subjects.

Finally, we focus on the results for the uneven condition, comparing the percentage of decisions of two types, one representing the suboptimal one of choosing the most likely door 4 and sticking with it and the second the optimal one of choosing the least likely door 1 and switching away from it. The percentage of this type of sub-optimal choices began at 46% on block 1 but gradually decreased to 39% on block 2, 32% on block 3, 29% on block 4, 28% on block 5, and 26% on block 6. The two types intersect between blocks 4 and 5. On blocks 5 and 6, subjects in the uneven condition were more likely to play the optimal strategy than this particular sub-optimal strategy which had been the modal strategy on trial 1.

Concluding Observations

Considering the pattern of responses across trials, it is clear that some improvement and learning take place. By the tough standard used, about one fifth of the subjects had mastered the problem by the time they had played the game for 60 trials. However, many of the other subjects reach a certain level of success, and that may be about what they expect or perhaps they feel they can do no better. The clearest evidence of satisficing appears as the plateau in the equal probability condition in Figure 13.1.

One reviewer of this experiment suggested an important distinction that can be made regarding the source of satisficing as being either perceptual or motivational. That is, some people may quit trying to improve because of their perception that further improvement is impossible or highly unlikely. Others may perceive that further improvement is possible but very costly in effort and resources. The data do not permit us to analyze which of these sources was responsible for satisficing that may have occurred among the subjects in the current study, but this is a distinction that deserves attention in the future.

People in the even condition of the present study who switch on every trial can expect to win on 75% of the trials, while those who switch on none of the trials win about 25% of the time. This difference should be large enough to be perceived. In fact, however, most subjects played a mixed strategy, and that makes it harder to perceive the difference. If subjects had been told that the optimum strategy is to either never switch or always switch, they might have been more likely to arrive at the best strategy of always switching.

Overall, there was a correlation of +.88 between the number of switches a subject made and the number of correct trials in the even probability condition. However, if a subject in that condition switched on 85% or 90% of the trials, it would probably be impossible to discern a difference in outcome from the optimal 100% switching strategy. Of course, even though we have been focusing on the subjects developing an optimal strategy through inductive learning, it is also possible to derive the optimal strategy through deductive reasoning.

In the present study, people were given feedback concerning their success or failure after each trial. In future studies, they could be given more anti-satisficing information. For instance, they could be told after each block of 10 trials whether they had found the optimal solution, and, if not, they could be encouraged to continue thinking about the problem and searching for the optimal solution. Generally, satisficing in problem solving can be reduced by making the problem less difficult or more tractable, by studying subjects with greater ability, or by increasing subjects' motivation. In general, then, if one is interested in satisficing, and how to counter it, the equal probability Monty Hall Dilemma with a large number of trials is recommended.

On the other hand, if one is interested in insightful learning, the Monty Hall Dilemma with unequal probabilities contains some attractive features. The optimal solution is by no means obvious on the initial exposure to the problem. However, if people happen to try the optimal solution, they are very likely—though still not certain—to experience a positive outcome. Whether they fully appreciate the solution at once, the positive feedback will help to insure that they repeat that strategy, and ultimately realize that they have found the optimal solution. Consequently, they will be more likely to persist in following the optimal strategy for the remainder of the trials. Somewhere along the line they may experience "Eureka." More insight into the thought processes of subjects in the Monty Hall Dilemma could be obtained by asking them to think aloud while playing the game.

The view that the Monty Hall Dilemma with unequal probabilities is better suited for studying insightful learning gains some support in the current study. Specifically, people in the uneven condition were more likely to follow the pattern of never using the optimal solution up to a certain point and then always using it thereafter. People in the uneven condition were also more likely to claim that they had used a strategy during the 60 trial game. Anecdotally, several people in the uneven probability condition volunteered to play the entire game a second time. Although the experimenter said, "No thanks" to this offer, these subjects seemed convinced that they now knew the optimal solution and that by using it from the outset, they could rack up a very high score the second time around.

PART THREE

Odds and Ends

CHAPTER 14
CONTEXT EFFECT

One of the common criticisms about the Monty Hall Dilemma is that it has no meaningful context or substance. It is said to have no precise counterpart in real-life, and, therefore, people have no prior experience to draw upon when participating in an experiment or survey. The counterargument is that the Monty Hall Dilemma provides a setting in which to study two-stage decision making where there is a correct solution. This is often not the case with real-life decisions, of the two-stage variety e.g., when a couple decides to buy a house, then receives more information, and then makes a final decision. How can one tell if their decision is "correct?"

Nonetheless, we searched for a way to pose the Monty Hall Dilemma so that it would seem more realistic and resemble more closely real-life decision making. Our hypothesis was that providing people with a realistic context or frame would make it even more likely that they would stick with their initial answer. In a more engaging, content-laden, situation, people have more to cling to than in the standard Monty Hall Dilemma.

Tiffany Julian and I decided to use a modified vocabulary test. It would be similar to the type of standard multiple choice exam format used extensively by high school and college students in the U.S.

Imagine the situation faced by a participant. I am given a rather difficult vocabulary word that I may have seen before but am unsure as to its meaning. Four alternative meanings are provided, only one of which is correct. After I make a preliminary guess, the host eliminates two of the incorrect alternatives. I think to myself, "Thus far, my initial guess has not been shown to be wrong, while two others have been shown to be incorrect." In such a situation, a person may be even less inclined to switch than someone answering the usual content-free question about doors.

Creating a New Context Condition

In the pre-test phase of this study, participants were 73 students in an undergraduate social psychology class at the University of Missouri. A pool of 107 vocabulary items was selected from the "It Pays to Increase Your Word Power" section of the *Reader's Digest*. They were selected to be difficult items but ones that the subjects might sense that they had seen or heard before. When these items were pre-tested, students were told that the two people with the highest number correct would each win a pizza.

For the experiment, we wanted difficult words that only 1/4 to 1/3 of the people would get right. After looking at the pre-test results, the range was expanded by 5 percentage points in either direction. Thus, the item could be chosen for the experiment if between 20% and 38% got it right.

Each participant was assigned randomly by the computer to either a STANDARD 4 door Monty Hall Dilemma (N=46) or to the WORD condition (N=35) involving the vocabulary test. For the WORD condition subjects made an initial guess, and then the computer showed them two incorrect words. Then the subjects made a final guess. This procedure was followed for 50 trials. The control condition was a standard four door Monty Hall Dilemma with no mention of a vocabulary test.

The Effect of the Vocabulary Context

The evidence summarized in Table 14.1 indicates that, as hypothesized, participants in the WORD condition did indeed switch less across trials. Overall the average number of switches was 21.5 for the WORD condition, compared to 28.0 (out of 50) for the STANDARD condition. This difference is statistically significant. Breaking that down into five blocks of 10 trials each, participants in the STANDARD condition switched more than participants in the WORD condition on each of the five blocks.

Table 14.1

Average Number of Switches Under Two Conditions

Condition	Trials					
	1-10	11-20	21-30	31-40	41-50	Overall
Standard	3.3	5.3	6.5	6.4	6.5	28.0
Vocabulary	2.2	4.4	4.2	5.3	5.4	21.3

Note: The possible range for each block of 10 trials is 0-10.

Looking at the first and last trials, 6% (2/35) in the WORD condition switched on the first trial, compared to 11% (5/46) in the STANDARD condition. Nearly half (17/35, 49%) of the participants in the WORD condition switched on trial 50, compared to 61% (28/46) in the STANDARD condition. There was a strong correlation within each condition between the number of switches and the number of correct answers. That correlation was +.90 for the WORD condition and +.87 for the STANDARD condition. If we invoke switching on each of the last 10 trials as measuring mastery of the problem, 20% in each condition (7/35 and 9/46) met this demanding criterion.

In summary, we have shown that presenting the Monty Hall Dilemma in a more meaningful context does not increase the amount of switching. In fact, the results were in the opposite direction. Subjects in the vocabulary condition actually switched less than subjects in the standard Monty Hall condition. Therefore, perhaps critics of the usual Monty Hall format must devise some other line of criticism besides its contrived and unusual nature.

CHAPTER 15

PROBABILITY AND ODDS

Some Examples of Misuse

One thing became abundantly clear while reading the letters to Marilyn vos Savant regarding the Monty Hall Dilemma. There are many letter writers out there who do not understand the basic distinction between probability and odds. Once this became apparent to me, I began to notice confusion and error on this point in many places, including some people in high positions with lofty credentials.

Let us begin here with a simple example. If I draw a card at random from a full deck of cards, excluding the jokers, the probability of that card being a heart is 1/4, but the odds are not 1:4, but rather 1:3. The **probability** of a positive event occurring is the number of positive events over the total number of events (positive or negative). The **odds** of a positive event occurring are the number of positive events divided by the number of negative events. Thus, the probability of a playing card being a heart is 13/52 or 1/4, and the probability of it not being a heart is 39/52 or 3/4. On the other hand, the odds of a playing card being a heart are 13:39 or 1:3. The odds of it not being a heart are 39:13 or 3:1.

My impression is that confusion over this rather basic distinction is pervasive. Even the New York State Lottery got it wrong, giving the probability of winning but calling it odds. A front and back copy of a New York State Lottery ticket was sent to me by Gregory Forbes, a high school math teacher in North Dakota.

A. K. Dewdny wrote a column in **Scientific American** for many years, as well as a fascinating book, **200% of Nothing**. However, in that book, he used the distinction between odds and probability incorrectly, as evidenced in the following excerpt:

> In January 1991, the American Cancer Society announced that the odds of women getting breast cancer had risen to one in nine. Women all over North America panicked at the one-ninth proba- bility, saying to themselves in effect, "Of course, I would just be the one!" . . . Women, understandably, imagined that the probability applied to themselves sometime soon, when, in fact, it didn't. . . . [T]he one-ninth probability applied over an entire lifetime—a 110- year lifetime. The probability of a woman dying, sooner or later, of breast cancer is one-ninth or about 0.11. For a woman under 50, the chance over the next year is more like 1 in 1,000.[1]

In addition to the incorrect use of odds, there is some confusion about whether the one in nine probability referred to "getting breast cancer" or to dying from breast cancer. Surely the latter would be associated with longer odds than the former. A similar error was made by Scott Plous in his award- winning book, **The Psychology of Judgment and Decision Making**, "Suppose you are a physician who had just examined a woman for breast cancer. The woman has a lump in her breast, but based on many years of experience, you estimate the odds of a malignancy as one in a hundred."[2] It should be that the probability is 1/100 or that the odds are 1:99. Next we consider an excerpt from an article by Jerry Burger and Harris Cooper, published in the psychology journal, **Motivation and Emotion:**

---

1 A. K. Dewdny, **200% of Nothing**, 1993, New York: John Wiley.
2 S. Plous, **The Psychology of Judgment and Decision Making**. 1993, New York: McGraw-Hill.

It was then explained to all subjects that they were to bet on whether or not the numbers on a pair of dice would add up to a certain number. . . . The target numbers were presented in the same order for all subjects and the payoff ratios were legitimate chance figures (for example, the chance of throwing a 9 is 1 to 9, and a 9-to-1 payoff ratio was used for this number.)[3]

In fact, the chance of throwing a 9 is 1 in 9, or to say it differently, the odds of throwing a 9 are 1:8. If "the house" paid 9 dollars every time the subject rolled a 9, and collected 1 dollar every time a non-9 was rolled, the house would lose money in the long run. If the house paid 8 dollars every time a 9 was rolled and collected 1 dollar each time a non-9 was rolled, the house would break even in the long run.

In standard roulette, there are 18 red slots, 18 black slots, and 2 green slots. The probability of the ball landing in a red number is 18/38 (about .474), but the odds are 18:20, or 9:10. If a player bets on the ball landing on any red number, and the house pays even ($1 payoff for each $1 bet), you can see that in the long run, the house is destined to win. It is the possibility of the ball landing on green that gives the house the edge.

Back to the Monty Hall Dilemma

With the preceding as background, let us return to the Monty Hall Dilemma, and consider a portion of Marilyn's second column on the subject, in which she addressed her critics:

My original answer is correct. But first, let me explain why your answer is wrong. **The winning odds of 1/3 on the first choice can't go up to 1/2 just because the host opens a losing door.** To illustrate this, let's say we play a shell game. You look away, and I put a pea under one of three shells. Then I ask you to put your finger on a shell. **The odds that your choice contains a pea are 1/3, agreed?**

---

3 J. M. Burger and H. M. Cooper, "The desirability of control," **Motivation and Emotion,** 1979, **3,** No. 4, 381-393.

Then I simply lift up an empty shell from the remaining two. As I can (and will) do this regardless of what you've chosen, we've learned nothing to allow us to revise the odds on the shell under your finger.

The highlighted sentences are incorrect and should have read, "The winning odds of 1:2 can't go up to 1:1 just because the host opens a losing door." And "The odds that your choice contains a pea are 1:2, agreed?"

Of the people who wrote a letter to Marilyn vos Savant, in response to her second column, there were at least 10 critics who pointed out this error. Several of them were high school math teachers. Nonetheless, a very large majority of the letter writers who used the terms, odds, probability, and chance were incorrect in their usage. Part of this may have stemmed from the way vos Savant framed her commentary. That is, the critical letter writers may have taken on the style and usage from vos Savant's incorrect wording. However, it may also be that many people have an incorrect notion about odds and probability. To her credit, when she published the column in book form some 6 years later, her usage was corrected.[4]

A New Word Problem on Probability and Odds

For a questionnaire study done by Marcia Wisdom at Missouri Valley College, we devised an item designed to provide a basis for teaching the distinction between odds and probability. The wording of the question went as follows:

Pat and Terry take turns rolling a pair of dice for 200 turns (100 rolls each). After each roll, if any double (2 ones, 2 twos, 2 threes, 2 fours, 2 fives, or 2 sixes) is showing, Pat pays Terry $6. If not, Terry pays Pat $1.

Note: Each die can be 1, 2, 3, 4, 5, or 6; therefore, there are 36 different ways the pair of dice can turn out on a given roll (6 x 6).

Over the 200 rolls, which outcome is most likely?
(Circle one.)

---

4 M. vos Savant, **The Power of Logical Thinking**. 1996, New York: St. Martin's Press, p. 7.

a. Pat will win more money than Terry.

b. Pat and Terry will come out exactly even.

c. Terry and Pat have even odds, but it is not likely they will come out exactly even. One of them will win, but it can't be stated in advance which one.

d. Terry will win more money that Pat.

The probability of a double on any given roll is 1/6. However, the odds of rolling a double are 1:5, not 1:6. Therefore, the expected value for Terry over 200 rolls is $200 (200 hundred trials x 1/6 chance of winning on a given trial x $6 for each trial in which a double is thrown). On the other hand, the expected value for Pat is about $167 (200 trials x 5/6 chance of winning on a given trial x $1 for each trial on which a double is not thrown). If the rules were changed so that Terry was paid $5, corresponding to the odds rather than the probability, the expected value for Pat and Terry would be the same and c. would have been the correct answer. As the questions stands, the correct answer is d. The correct answer was obtained by only 18%, somewhat less than would be expected if people randomly selected an answer (25%). Overall, of the 441 undergraduate students who answered the question, 19% chose a., 7% chose b., 56% chose c., and 18% chose d.

Who Wouldn't Want to be a Millionaire?

In 1999, the ABC television network began a new show in the U.S., "Who Wants to be a Millionaire?" This show was apparently copied from a popular British quiz show. The U.S. version was hosted by Regis Philbin, and contestants who passed several preliminary contests, could then win a million dollars by answering correctly 15 consecutive multiple choice questions.

The show differed from another popular TV quiz show from a few decades back, "The $64,000 Question," in some interesting ways. On the latter, people chose a specific topic, e.g., opera, boxing, Shakespeare, and had to answer only questions pertaining to that topic. On "Who Wants to be a Millionaire," contestants had no choice about the category or subject matter. However, on "The $64,000 Question," people had to answer open ended questions (recall rather than mere recognition), a more difficult task.

On "Who Wants to be a Millionaire," people answer multiple choice questions by selecting among four alternatives. Thus, it is possible that one could go all the way, choosing the answer at random, but that would be most unlikely. (The probability of doing that would be 1/4 to the 15th power, or about .0000000000931.) Another difference is that on the $64,000 question, the contestant had to choose whether to continue before being given the question. On "Who Wants to be a Millionaire," the contestant hears the next question before deciding whether to attempt an answer; the contestant can quit at any point and is eliminated only by giving the wrong answer or voluntarily deciding to quit at some point. Both shows had plateaus where the contestant could be assured of winning no less than a certain amount (for "Who Wants to be a Millionaire," the plateaus were at $1,000 and $32,000).

A couple of special features of "Who Wants to be a Millionaire" are of interest here. First, the host asks routinely, "Is that your final answer?" after the contestant gives a preliminary answer. Nearly always, the contestant replies, "Yes, it is." This implies a two-stage decision, preliminary and final, but consistent with the research on the Monty Hall Dilemma, the contestant almost never changes an answer at that point. That is understandable, given that no new information is provided, but we don't know what goes on in the minds of contestants.

Second, and of greater interest, is the use of "life-lines" on "Who Wants to be a Millionaire." In the course of attempting to answer the 15 questions, the contestant has the option of using three life-lines to obtain assistance. One can phone one of five designated friends, poll the audience to see how they would answer the question (at one point the host stated that at least a plurality of the audience was correct in 94% of the cases), and 50:50 in which two of the three wrong answers for a particular item are eliminated. Each life-line can be used only once, but the contestant can use more than one life-line for a given question.

"50:50" seems to be a satisfactory way of referring to the odds of answering, at random, the question correctly after using that life-line. Another way is to say that by chance, the initial probability was 1/4, and that changes to 1/2 after two incorrect answers are eliminated. However, it would be desirable to know how the two wrong answers are selected to be eliminated. On the show, the host simply says, "OK, let's ask the computer to eliminate two wrong answers," without specifying how the wrong answers to be eliminated are chosen. The computer could be programmed to select two of the three incorrect answers at random to be eliminated. However, it could also be programmed to eliminate the two most unlikely answers, based on some pre-test of the items. For us to declare that the odds are really 50:50 (1:1), we would want to know how the wrong answers to be eliminated are chosen, and that is not stated by the host or in the rules of the game which were posted on the show's website.

So what is the difference between a 4-door Monty Hall Dilemma, where the odds are 1:3 of winning by sticking with one's initial hunch, and the 50:50 life-line on "Who Wants to Be a Millionaire?" where the odds are 1:1? In the Monty Hall Dilemma, the contestant would indicate a preliminary answer, and that alternative would not be eliminated by the host. Rather, the host would eliminate 2 of the other 3 answers, and in the event that the contestant's initial selection was the correct answer, the host would choose randomly 2 of the 3 alternatives to be eliminated. If the contestant's initial answer was incorrect, the host would eliminate the other two incorrect answers, avoiding the correct answer as well as the contestant's initial answer. Then the contestant can choose to stick with a probability of winning at 1/4 or switch to the remaining answer with a probability of winning at 3/4.

That is the situation for the contestant who really doesn't know the answer and has no basis for differentiating among the alternatives. If the contestant can differentiate the alternative answers, attaching some subjective probability to each of them, then the correct strategy would be to select the least likely alternative and switch away from it.

In the 50:50 life-line, on the other hand, the contestant is not asked to make a preliminary guess. If the contestant nonetheless does so, this presumably does not affect the two wrong answers to be eliminated "by the computer." So, if the contestant does have a tentative answer, it still could be one of the two wrong answers that are eliminated by the computer. In the Monty Hall Dilemma, the preliminary choice is an important part of the process, i.e., it is consequential for the train of events that follows. In the 50:50 life-line on "Who Wants to be a Millionaire," a preliminary guess is neither a necessary part of the process nor is it consequential.

Switching and Sticking on Multiple Choice Exams

One day, many years ago, I was trying to solve a problem on the blackboard in a high school math class. I had the correct answer, but then I erased the correct solution and continued working on the problem until I got it wrong. The teacher stood by patiently, but she finally not only corrected my mistake, but also admonished me by one of her many proverbs, "Donald, your first thought is generally correct."

That incident often came back to me when I heard this advice given as the proper strategy for taking multiple choice exams. In one of our experiments, I included a statement, "My first thought is generally correct." Of those expressing an opinion, 79% agreed, and this was just **after** they had played 50 trials of the Monty Hall Dilemma, in which their first answer was incorrect more often than not. I have wondered what is the basis for such beliefs. Is it grounded in some solid research, or is it just a widely held cultural myth? I have asked many colleagues in psychology, especially those involved with tests and measurements. I have challenged students, both graduate and undergraduate, to document the basis of that belief. But so far it has been to no avail.

Professor Steven Wise of the University of Nebraska directed me to a body of literature in the field of educational psychology, dating back as far as the 1920s and extending into the 1990s. That research has focused on instances in which people have actually changed their answers on multiple choice exams. Study after study indicated that people make changes from wrong to right more often than changes from right to wrong by a ratio of more than 2:1. That ratio is not fixed in that if the students began to change their answers more often (or less often) than they currently do, the ratio could change.

It could be that instances in which students change from a right answer to a wrong one are particularly salient in the minds of students because it may have caused them to be just short of a higher grade on the exam. In any event, we tried to tap into the impression derived by students. In two surveys, the first at the University of Missouri, and the second at Missouri Valley College, undergraduates answered this question:

> On multiple choice tests, people are often uncertain about which answer is correct and must decide whether to stick with their first answer or switch to another answer. If we limit consideration to questions on which there is just one correct answer, there are only three possibilities. People can switch from a right answer to a wrong answer, from a wrong answer to a right answer, or from one wrong answer to another wrong answer. Please give your estimates as to how frequently each of these types occurs both in terms of your own personal experience as it has happened to you, and in terms of how you think it happens to undergraduate test-takers in general.

As shown in Table 15.1, the estimates given by respondents at the two schools are quite similar. In both surveys, respondents estimated that the most common type of change would be switch from a right answer to a wrong answer. Respondents gave significantly higher estimates for the right to wrong type than for either of the other two types. This may indicate their perceptions or impressions, but the actual evidence from objective research does not support their claims.

Table 15.1

Estimates of Types of Errors on Multiple Choice Tests

	Average Percent Estimated			
	Your Own Experience		Undergraduate Test Taking	
Switch From	University of Missouri	Missouri Valley College	University of Missouri	Missouri Valley College
Right to Wrong	41.3	41.3	41.1	41.6
Wrong to Right	34.9	32.9	32.8	33.2
Wrong to Wrong	23.4	26.7	25.8	27.2
Sum	99.5	100.9	98.9	101.0

Note: The number of respondents was 341 for the University of Missouri and 418 for Missouri Valley College. The wording of the question is given in the text. The sum of the three averages should total 100, since the three alternatives are mutually exclusive and mutually exhaustive. This was indicated on the questionnaire, but nonetheless, some respondents gave estimates that do not add up to 100.

The source of the idea that one's first answer is generally correct remains a mystery, but it is quite pervasive. Most people, including some whose profession might indicate otherwise, find odds and probability to be rather baffling. Approaching the Monty Hall Dilemma without much confidence in dealing with odds and probability may instill a reluctance to abandon the status quo. The status quo is created when people make their initial choice, and the conservative impulse may impel people to be inclined to stick with an initial answer rather than switch in one's final answer.

Epilogue

"No epilogue I pray you. For your play needs no excuse."

Theseus addressing the Rustics in Act V, Scene 1 in William Shakespeare's *A Midsummer Night's Dream.*

But if I were to have an epilogue, what sorts of things would I want to include? First, the Monty Hall Dilemma is best understood as a cognitive illusion with an explicit set of assumptions. It does involve a two stage decision process, but not all two stage decisions meet the criteria of a Monty Hall Dilemma. Similarly, while the Monty Hall Dilemma is a cognitive illusion, not all cognitive illusions are Monty Hall Dilemmas. In the prisoner's dilemma, the choice is whether to confess or not to confess; in the game of chicken, the choice is to swerve or not to swerve; in the Monty Hall Dilemma, the contestant decides to stick or switch.

There is a pervasive tendency for people to stick when on rational grounds, they should switch. Some people experience frustration and anger over the Monty Hall Dilemma. This tendency to stick extends to students in four very different cultures, thus providing evidence of a finding with considerable generality. When people play the Monty Hall Dilemma over several trials, they show signs of learning that switching is beneficial. However, following an initial increase from about 10% to about 55%

switching, they reach a plateau. People show signs of satisficing across trials. Also, they approach the Monty Hall Dilemma as if it involved uncertainty whereas it really is a risk situation. The illusion of control, belief perseverance, status quo bias, and psychological commitment are among the social psychological concepts that may be relevant to a more complete understanding of this intriguing phenomenon.

Appendix A

Marilyn vos Savant's Four Columns on the Monty Hall Dilemma

Ask Marilyn™
BY MARILYN VOS SAVANT

Suppose you're on a game show, and you're given the choice of three doors: Behind one door is a car; behind the others, goats. You pick a door, say No. 1, and the host, who knows what's behind the doors, opens another door, say No. 3, which has a goat. He then says to you, "Do you want to pick door No. 2?" Is it to your advantage to switch your choice?
—Craig F. Whitaker,
Columbia, Md.

Yes; you should switch. The first door has a one-third chance of winning, but the second door has a two-thirds chance. Here's a good way to visualize what happened. Suppose there are a *million* doors, and you pick door No. 1. Then the host, who knows what's behind the doors and will always avoid the one with the prize, opens them all except door #777,777, You'd switch to that door pretty fast, wouldn't you?

PARADE MAGAZINE · SEPTEMBER 9, 1990

Ask Marilyn™
BY MARILYN VOS SAVANT

I'll come straight to the point. In the following question and answer, you blew it!

"Suppose you're on a game show and given a choice of three doors. Behind one is a car; behind the others are goats. You pick Door No. 1, and the host, who knows what's behind them, opens No. 3, which has a goat. He then asks if you want to pick No. 2. Should you switch?"

You answered, "Yes. The first door has a 1/3 chance of winning, but the second has a 2/3 chance."

Let me explain: If one door is shown to be a loser, that information changes the probability to 1/2. As a professional mathematician, I'm very concerned with the general public's lack of mathematical skills. Please help by confessing your error and, in the future, being more careful.

—Robert Sachs, Ph.D.,
George Mason University,
Fairfax, Va.

You blew it, and you blew it big! I'll explain: After the host reveals a goat, you now have a one-in-two chance of being correct. Whether you change your answer or not, the odds are the same. There is enough mathematical illiteracy in this country, and we don't need the world's highest IQ propagating more. Shame!

—Scott Smith, Ph.D.,
University of Florida

Your answer to the question is in error. But if it is any consolation, many of my academic colleagues also have been stumped by this problem.

—Barry Pasternack, Ph.D.,
California Faculty Association

Good heavens! With so much learned opposition, I'll bet this one is going to keep math classes all over the country busy on Monday.

My original answer is correct. But first, let me explain why your answer is wrong. The winning odds of 1/3 on the first choice can't go up to 1/2 just because the host opens a losing door. To illustrate this, let's say we play a shell game. You look away, and I put a pea under one of three shells. Then I ask you to put your finger on a shell. The odds that your choice contains a pea are 1/3, agreed? Then I simply lift up an empty shell from the remaining two. As I can (and will) do this regardless of what you've chosen, we've learned nothing to allow us to revise the odds on the shell under your finger.

The benefits of switching are readily proved by playing through the six games that exhaust all the possibilities. For the first three games, you choose No. 1 and switch each time; for the second three games, you choose No. 1 and "stay" each time, and the host always opens a loser. Here are the results (each row is a game):

DOOR 1	DOOR 2	DOOR 3
AUTO Switch and you lose.	GOAT	GOAT
GOAT Switch and you win.	AUTO	GOAT
GOAT Switch and you win.	GOAT	AUTO
AUTO Stay and you win.	GOAT	GOAT
GOAT Stay and you lose.	AUTO	GOAT
GOAT Stay and you lose.	GOAT	AUTO

When you switch, you win two out of three times and lose one time in three; but when you don't switch, you only win one in three times.

You can play the game with another person acting as host with three playing cards—two jokers for the goats and an ace for the auto. Doing it a few hundred times to get valid statistics can get a little tedious, so perhaps you can assign it for extra credit—or for punishment. (*That'll* get their goats!)

PARADE MAGAZINE · DECEMBER 2, 1990

Ask Marilyn™
BY MARILYN VOS SAVANT

You are in error—and you have ignored good counsel—but Albert Einstein earned a dearer place in the hearts of the people after he admitted his errors.

—Frank Rose, Ph.D., University of Michigan

I have been a faithful reader of your column and have not, until now, had any reason to doubt you. However, in this matter, in which I do have expertise, your answer is clearly at odds with the truth.

—James Rauff, Ph.D,
Millikin University

May I suggest that you obtain and refer to a standard textbook on probability before you try to answer a question of this type again?

—Charles Reid, Ph.D.,
University of Florida

Your logic is in error, and I am sure you will receive many letters on this topic from high school and college students. Perhaps you should keep a few addresses for help with future columns.

—W. Robert Smith, Ph.D.,
Georgia State University

You are utterly incorrect about the game-show question, and I hope this controversy will call some public attention to the serious national crisis in mathematical education. If you can admit your error, you will have contributed constructively toward the solution of a deplorable situation. How many irate mathematicians are needed to get you to change your mind?

—E. Ray Bobo, Ph.D.,
Georgetown University

I am in shock that after being corrected by at least three mathematicians, you still do not see your mistake.

—Kent Ford,
Dickinson State University

Maybe women look at math problems differently than men.

—Don Edwards, Sunriver, Ore.

You are the goat!

—Glenn Calkins
Western State College

You're wrong, but look at the positive side. If all those Ph.D.s were wrong, the country would be in very serious trouble.

—Everett Harman, Ph.D.,
U.S. Army Research Institute

Gasp! If this controversy continues, even the *postman* won't be able to fit into the mailroom. I'm receiving thousands of letters, nearly all insisting that I'm wrong, including one from the deputy director of the Center for Defense Information and another from a research mathematical statistician from the National Institutes of Health! Of the letters from the general public, 92% are against my answer; and of the letters from universities, 65% are against my answer. Overall, nine out of 10 readers completely disagree with my reply.

But math answers aren't determined by votes. For those readers new to all this, here's the original question and answer in full to which the first readers responded:

"Suppose you're on a game show, and you're given a choice of three doors. Behind one door is a car; behind the others, goats. You pick a door—say, No. 1—and the host, who knows what's behind the doors, opens another door—say, No. 3—which has a goat. He then says to you, 'Do you want to pick door No. 2?' Is it to your advantage to switch your choice?"

I answered, "Yes, you should switch. The first door has a 1/3 chance of winning, but the second door has a 2/3 chance. Here's a good way to visualize what happened. Suppose there are a *million* doors, and you pick door No. 1. Then the host, who knows what's behind the doors and will always avoid the one with the prize, opens them all except door No. 777,777. You'd switch to that door pretty fast, wouldn't you?"

So many readers wrote to say they thought there was *no* advantage to switching (and that the chances became equal) that we published a second explanatory column, affirming the correctness of the original reply and using a shell game and a probability grid as illustrations.

Now we're receiving far *more* mail, and even newspaper columnists are joining in the fray. The day after the second column appeared, lights started flashing here at the magazine. Telephone calls poured into the switchboard, fax machines churned out copy, and the mailroom began to sink under its own weight. Incredulous at the response, we read wild accusations of intellectual irresponsibility and, as the days went by, we were even more incredulous to read embarrassed retractions from some of those same people!

The reaction is understandable. When reality clashes so violently with intuition, people are shaken.

But understanding is strength, so let's look at it again, remembering that the original answer defines certain conditions—the most significant of which is that *the host will always open a losing door on purpose.* (There is no way he can always open a losing door by chance!) Anything else is a different question.

The original answer is still correct and the key to it lies in the question: *Should you switch?*

Suppose we pause at that point, and a UFO settles down onto this stage. A little green woman emerges, and the host asks her to point to one of the two unopened doors. The chances that *she'll* randomly choose the one with the prize are 1/2. But that's because she lacks the advantage the *original* contestant had—the help of the host. (Try to forget any particular television show.)

When you first choose door No. 1 from among the three, there's a 1/3 chance that the prize is behind that one and a 2/3 chance that it's behind one of the others. *But then the host steps in and gives you a clue.* If the prize is behind No. 2, the host shows you No. 3;

and if the prize is behind No. 3, the host shows you No. 2. So when you switch, you win if the prize is behind No. 2 *or* No. 3. *YOU WIN EITHER WAY!* But if you *don't* switch, you win only if the prize is behind door No. 1.

And as this problem is of such intense interest, I'm willing to put my thinking to the test with a nationwide experiment. This is a call to math classes all across the country. Set up a probability trial exactly as outlined below and send me a chart of all the games, along with a cover letter repeating just how you did it, so we can make sure the methods are consistent.

One student plays the contestant, another plays the host. Label three paper cups No. 1, No. 2, and No. 3. While the contestant looks away, the host randomly hides a penny under a cup by throwing a die until a 1, 2 or 3 comes up. Next, the contestant randomly points to a cup by throwing a die the same way. Then the host purposely lifts up a losing cup from the two unchosen. Last, the contestant "stays" and lifts up his original cup to see if it covers the penny. Play "not switching" 200 times and keep track of how often the contestant wins.

Then test the other strategy. Play the game the same way until the last instruction, at which point the contestant instead "switches" and lifts up the cup *not* chosen by anyone to see if it covers the penny. Play "switching" 200 times also.

And, here's one last letter:

Dear Marilyn:
You are indeed correct. My colleagues at work had a ball with this problem, and I dare say that most of them—including me at first—thought you were wrong!
　　　　—Seth Kalson, Ph.D.,
　　　　Massachusetts Institute of
　　　　Technology

Thanks, MIT. I needed that!

PARADE MAGAZINE · FEBRUARY 17, 1991

Ask Marilyn™
BY MARILYN VOS SAVANT

In a recent column, you called on math classes around the country to perform an experiment that would confirm your response to a game-show problem. ["Suppose you're on a game show, and you're given the choice of three doors. Behind one door is a car; behind the others, goats. You pick a door, say No. 1, and the host, who knows what's behind the doors, opens another door, say No. 3, which has a goat. He then says to you, 'Do you want to pick door No. 2?' Is it to your advantage to switch your choice?"]

You answered, "Yes, you should switch. The first door has a 1/3 chance of winning, but the second door has a 2/3 chance. Here's a good way to visualize what happened: Suppose there are a *million* doors, and you pick door No. 1. Then the host, who knows what's behind the doors and will always avoid the one with the prize, opens them all except door No. 777,777. You'd switch to that door pretty fast, wouldn't you?"

My eighth-grade classes tried it [switching and not switching, 200 times each using three cups and a coin]. I don't really understand how to set up an equation for your theory, but it definitely does work! You'll have to help rewrite the chapters on probability.
　　　　—Pat Gross, Ascension School,
　　　　Chesterfield, Mo.

Our class, with unbridled enthusiasm, is proud to announce that our data support your position. Thank you so much for your faith in America's educators to solve this.

—Jackie Charles,
Henry Grady Elementary,
Tampa, Fla.

My class had a great time watching your theory come to life. I wish you could have been here to witness it. Their joy is what makes teaching worthwhile.

—Pat Pascoli, Park View School
Wheeling, W.Va.

Seven groups worked on the probability problem. The numbers were impressive, and the students were astounded.

—R. Burrichter,
Webster Elementary School,
St Paul, MN

The best part was seeing the looks on the students' faces as their numbers were tallied. The results were thrilling!

—Patricia Robinson,
Ridge High School,
Basking Ridge, N.J.

You could hear the kids gasp, one at a time, "Oh, my gosh! She was right!"

—Jane Griffith,
Magnolia School, Oakdale,
Calif.

I must admit I doubted you until my fifth-grade math class proved you right. All I can say is WOW!

—John Witt,
Westside Elementary,
River Falls, Wis.

My classes enjoyed this and look forward to the next project you give America's students. This is the stuff of real science.

—Jerome Yeutter,
Hebron Public Schools,
Hebron, Neb.

Thanks for that fun math problem. I really enjoyed it. It got me out of fractions for two days! Have any more?

—Andrew Malinoski
Mabelle Avery School,
Sommers, Conn.

I did your experiment on probability as part of a science-fair project, and after extensive interviews with the judges, I was awarded first place.

—Adrienne Shelton,
Holy Spirit School,
Annandale, Va

I also thought you were wrong, so I did your experiment, and you were exactly correct. (I used three cups to represent the three doors, but instead of a penny I chose an aspirin tablet because I thought I might need to take it after my experiment.)

—William Hunt, M.D.,
West Palm Beach, Fla.

I put my solution of the problem on the bulletin board in the Physics Department office here, following it with a declaration that you were right. All morning I took a lot of criticism and abuse from my colleagues, but by late in the afternoon most of them came around. I even won a free dinner from one overconfident professor.

—Eugene Mosca, Ph.D., U.S.
Naval Academy, Annapolis, Md.

After considerable discussion and vacillation here at the Los Alamos National Laboratory, two of my colleagues independently programmed the problem, and in one million trials, switching paid off 66.7% of the time. The total running time on the computer was less than one second.

—G.P. DeVault, Ph.D.,
Los Alamos National Laboratory,
Los Alamos, N.M.

Now fess up. Did you really figure all this out, or did you get help from a mathematician?

—Lawrence Bryan,
San Jose, Calif.

Wow! What a response we received! It's still coming in, but so many of you are so anxious to hear the results that we'll stop tallying for a moment and take stock of the situation so far. We've received thousands of letters, and of the people who performed the experiment by hand as described, the results were close to unanimous: You win twice as often when you change doors. Nearly 100% of those readers now believe it pays to switch. But many people tried performing similar experiments on computers, fearlessly programming them in hundreds of different ways. Not surprisingly, they fared a little less well. Even so, about 97% of them now believe it pays to switch.

And plenty of people who *didn't* perform the experiment wrote too. Of the general public, about 56% now believe you should switch, compared with only 8% before. From academic institutions, about 71% now believe you should switch, compared with only 35% before. (Many of them commented that it altered their thinking dramatically, especially about the state of mathematical education in this country.) And a very small percentage of readers feel convinced that the furor is resulting from people not realizing that the host is opening a losing door on purpose. (But they haven't read my mail! The great majority of people understand the conditions perfectly.)

And so we've made progress! Half of the readers whose letters were published in the previous columns have written to say they've changed their minds. But, of course...

Dear Marilyn:
I still think you're wrong. There is such a thing as female logic.
—Don Edwards, Sunriver, Ore.
Oh, hush now.

PARADE MAGAZINE · JULY 7, 1991

Appendix B

Two Letters to the Editor of *The American Statistician* by Steve Selvin

A PROBLEM IN PROBABILITY

It is "Let's Make a Deal"—a famous TV show starring Monty Hall.

Monty Hall: One of the three boxes labeled A, B, and C contains the keys to that new 1975 Lincoln Continental. The other two are empty. If you choose the box containing the keys, you win the car.

Contestant: Gasp!

Monty Hall: Select one of these boxes.

Contestant: I'll take box B.

Monty Hall: Now box A and box C are on the table and here is box B (contestant grips box B tightly). It is possible the car keys are in that box! I'll give you $100 for the box.

Contestant: No, thank you.

Monty Hall: How about $200?

Contestant: No!

Audience: No!!

Monty Hall: Remember that the probability of your box containing the keys to the car is 1/3 and the probability of your box being empty is 2/3. I'll give you $500.

Audience: No!!

Contestant: No, I think I'll keep this box.

Monty Hall: I'll do you a favor and open one of the remaining boxes on the table (he opens box A). It's empty! (Audience: applause). Now either box C or your box B contains the car keys. Since there are two boxes left, the probability of your box containing the keys is now 1/2. I'll give you $1000 cash for your box.

WAIT!!!!

Is Monty right? The contestant knows that at least one of the boxes on the table is empty. He now knows it was box A. Does this knowledge change his probability of having the box containing the keys from 1/3 to 1/2? One of the boxes on the table has to be empty. Has Monty done the contestant a favor by showing him which of the two boxes was empty? Is the probability of winning the car 1/2 or 1/3?

Contestant: I'll trade you my box B for box C on the table.

Monty Hall: That's weird!!

Hint: The contestant knows what he is doing!

Steve Selvin
School of Public Health
Univ. of California
Berkeley, CA 94720

Solution to "A Problem in Probability"

Certainly Monty Hall knows which box is the winner and, therefore, would not open the box containing the keys to the car. Consider all possible outcomes:

Keyes are in box	Contestant chooses box	Monty Hall opens box	Contestant switches	Result
A	A	B or C	A for B or C	loses
A	B	C	B for A	wins
A	C	B	C for A	wins
B	A	C	A for B	wins
B	B	A or C	B for A or C	loses
B	C	A	C for B	wins
C	A	B	A for C	wins
C	B	A	B for C	wins
C	C	A or B	C for A or B	loses

Enumeration shows probability of winning is 6/9 = 2/3. If the contestant does not switch boxes, then his probability of winning the car remains unchanged (1/3) after Monty Hall opens an additional box.

Selvin, S. (1975). Letters to the Editor. *The American Statistician*, **29,** 67.

ON THE MONTY HALL PROBLEM

I have received a number of letters commenting on my "Letter to the Editor" in the *American Statistician* of February 1975 entitled "A Problem in Probability." Several correspondents claim my answer is incorrect. The basis to my solution is that Monty Hall knows which box contains the keys and when he can open either of two boxes without exposing the keys, he chooses between them at random. An alternative solution to enumerating the mutually exclusive and equally likely outcomes is as follows:

A = event that keys are contained in box B

B = event that contestant chooses box B

C= event that Monty Hall opens box A

Then
P (keys in box B | contestant selects B and Monty opens A)

$$= P(A \mid BC) = P(ABC)/P(BC)$$

$$= P(C \mid AB)P(AB)/P(C \mid B)P(B)$$

$$= P(C \mid AB)P(B \mid A)P(A)/P(C \mid B)P(B)$$

$$= (1/2)(1/3)(1/3)/(1/2)(1/3)$$

$$1/3$$

If the contestant trades his box B for the unopened box on the table, his probability of winning the car is 2/3.

D. L. Ferguson presented a generalization of this problem for the case of n boxes, in which Monty Hall opens p boxes. In this situation, the probability the contestant wins when he switches boxes in $(n-1)/[n(n-p-1)]$.

Benjamin King pointed out the critical assumptions about Monty Hall's behavior that are necessary to solve the problem, and emphasized that "the prior distribution is not the only part of the probabilistic side of a decision problem that is subjective."

Monty Hall wrote and expressed that he was not "a student of statistics problems" but "the big hole in your argument is that once the first box is seen to be empty, the contestant cannot exchange his box." He continues to say, "Oh, and incidentally, after one [box] is seen to be empty, his chances are no longer 50/50 but remain what they were in the first place, one out of three. It just seems to the contestant that one box having been eliminated, he stands a better chance. Not so." I could not have said it better myself.

Steve Selvin
School of Public Health
Univ. of California
Berkeley, CA 94720

Selvin, S. (1975). Letters to the Editor. *The American Statistician*, **29**, 134.

Appendix C

Two Computer Programs by Joseph Heiser

```
program Contest;     (vos Savant Interpretation)

var
  Rand,i,j,Games,Win     :integer;
  Door                   :Array[1..3] of string[4];
  W                      :REAL;

begin
  Randomize;
  Games := 0;
  Win := 0;
  Repeat
    Door[2] := ''; Door[3] := '';
    I := Random(3) + 1;
    Door[I] := 'AUTO';
      Games := Games + 1;
      If (Door[2] = 'AUTO') or (Door[3] = 'AUTO') then Win := Win + 1;
  Until Games = 30000;
  Writeln('NUMBER OF GAMES':28,'ODDS OF WINNING CHOOSING DOOR 2':42);
  W := Win/30000;
  WRITELN(GAMES:22,W:32:3);
  END.
```

```
    Rand,i,j,Games,Win      :integer;
    Door                    :Array[1..3] of string[4];
    W                       :REAL;


begin
  Randomize;
  Games := 0;
  Win := 0;
  Repeat
    Door[2] := '';
    I := Random(3) + 1;
    Door[I] := 'AUTO';
    If I <> 3 then
    begin
      Games := Games + 1;
      If Door[2] = 'AUTO' then Win := Win + 1;
    end;
  Until Games = 30000;
  Writeln('NUMBER OF GAMES':28,'ODDS OF WINNING CHOOSING
  W := Win/30000;
  WRITELN(GAMES:22,W:32:3);
  END.
```

Appendix D

Four Versions of the Instructions in Word Problem Study

(Monty-Gnostic)
Suppose you are a contestant on a game show. The host, who is known to be completely honest, has placed a new car behind one of three doors and a goat behind each of the other doors. "First you point to a door," the host says. "Then I'll open one of the other doors and show that it has a goat. After I've shown you the goat, you make your final choice, and you win whatever is behind that door." You begin by pointing to a door, say door number 2. The host then shows you that door 1 has a goat. What would your final choice be? Would you stick with door 2 or switch to door 3?

(Monty-Agnostic)
Suppose you are a contestant on a game show. A new car has been placed behind one of three doors and a goat behind each of the other doors. The host, who is known to be completely honest, says, "First you write down a door. Then without knowing where the car is or your initial answer, I'll open a door at random. If I open a door other than your initial choice, then you get to decide your final choice between the two remaining doors, and you win whatever is behind that door." You begin by writing down a door, say number 2. The host then randomly chooses a door and opens door 1

which has a goat. Would you then stick with door number 2 or switch to door 3?

(Roulette-Gnostic)

Suppose you are a contestant on a game show. The host, who is known to be completely honest, has placed a new car behind each of two doors and a goat behind a third door. "First you point to a door," the host says. "Then I'll open one of the other doors and show that it has a car. That door will no longer be available to you. After I've shown you that door with a car, you make your final choice, and you win whatever is behind that door." You begin by pointing to a door, say door number 2. The host then shows you that door 1 has a car. What would your final choice be? Would you stick with door 2 or switch to door 3?

(Roulette-Agnostic)

Suppose you are a contestant on a game show. A new car has been placed behind each of two doors and a goat behind a third door. The host, who is known to be completely honest, says, "First you write down a door. Then without knowing where the cars are or your initial answer, I will open a door at random. If I open a door other than your initial choice, then you get to decide your final choice between the two remaining doors, and you win whatever is behind that door." You begin by writing down a door, say number 2. The host then randomly chooses a door and opens door 1 which has a car. Would you then stick with door number 2 or switch to door 3?

About the Author

Donald Granberg obtained his BA in psychology from Gustavus Adolphus College and his PhD in sociology from The Pennsylvania State University. He received an honorary doctorate from the University of Göteborg in Sweden. He served on the faculty at the University of Missouri for thirty-four years. He co-authored *The Political System Matters: Social Psychology and Voting Behavior in Sweden and the United States* **and** *A Most Human Enterprise: Controversies in the Social Sciences* **and co-edited** *Social Judgment and Intergroup Relations: Essays in Honor of Muzafer Sherif.*

About the Cover Illustrator

Pat Bagley is an award winning editorial illustrator and journalist for the *Salt Lake Tribune*, Salt Lake City, Utah.

11297312R00117

Printed in Great Britain
by Amazon